THE
Archive Photographs
SERIES

REDRUTH

UNDER ROYAL PATRONAGE.

B. EVES, AUTHOR.

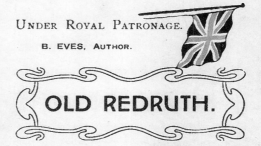

OLD REDRUTH.

Redruth ! This good old Rugged Town,
  For years and years, has been
The Home of the Cornish Miner
  And powerful Steam-engine.

Where lofty stacks smoke here and there
  Around on wild St. Day,
The Whim, and Shaft, and Metal Raff
  Heard rumbling night and day.

Fine buildings of great works display
  Their Engineering Skill,
With the Steam-saw, Drill and Hammer,
  The Moulder, and the Mill.

Down in rustic Lanner Village,
  Where cottages look gay,
Perfumed with the sweet old Lilac,
  And Haw-Thorn now in May, .

In pretty Portreath's sandy cove,
  The Sea-Gulls flock all day,
Some perched upon the rough gull rock,
  In feathers white and grey.

To the Monument and Castle
  The Lovers climb their way,
Here to view this Town and Country,
  O'er granite rough and grey.

Rare Ancestral Country Mansions,
  Adorned with wonderous art,
Nestled in their green plantations,
  Stand pleasantly apart.

A wheel fixed on the old Tin-Stream,
  Turns slowly in the Vale,
While the notes from a lonely Cuckoo,
  Charms all the wooded Dale,

May, 1918.]

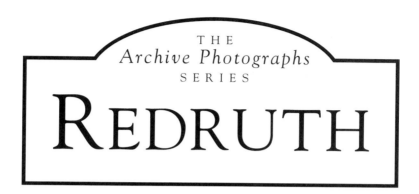

THE Archive Photographs SERIES

REDRUTH

Compiled by
Paddy Bradley

CHALFORD

The Chalford Publishing Company
St Mary's Mill, Chalford,
Stroud, Gloucestershire, GL6 8NX

ISBN 0 7524 0304 4

Typesetting and origination by
The Chalford Publishing Company
Printed in Great Britain by
Redwood Books, Trowbridge

*To my wife Margaret
whose love, understanding and patience
has made this possible.*

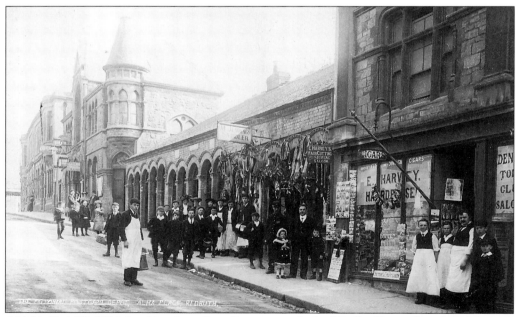

ALMA PLACE 1905. Looking from Fore Street towards the "Coffee Tavern", with E. Harvey's hairdressing shop and "Monty' Jennings saddlery business in the foreground.

Contents

Acknowledgements

I would like to express my sincere thanks to all those who have given me valuable assistance in compiling this book.

Don and Joan Pethick, Margaret and Frank Bray, Richard and Jean Eathorne, Mrs Joy Millington, Miss Florence Paul, Percy Hailey, Clifford Harris, Tony Clarke, Paul Annear, Mrs Marjorie Collins, Mrs Marie Trevithick, Mrs Pearl Gunn, Mr David Reed, Mrs Muriel Fletcher, Donovan and Margaret Wilkins, Mr Jack Trounson (Dec'd), Mr Frank Mitchell for allowing me to use information from his own book, Mr John Watton for reproducing some of the photographs, Mr Terry Knight and his staff at the Cornish Studies Library at Redruth and last but not least my son, David, and daughter-in-law, Prue, without whose help and expertise on the typewriter this would not have been possible.

If there is anyone I have overlooked, please accept my deepest apologies.

Introduction

Over many years I have gained a great deal of pleasure and satisfaction in collecting old photographs and postcards of Redruth and the surrounding district. When I was asked to produce a book of the area I was delighted to accept. I felt it was a way for me to say "thank you" to those people who, over the years, kindly let me have photographs and postcards that help form a pictorial history of days gone by.

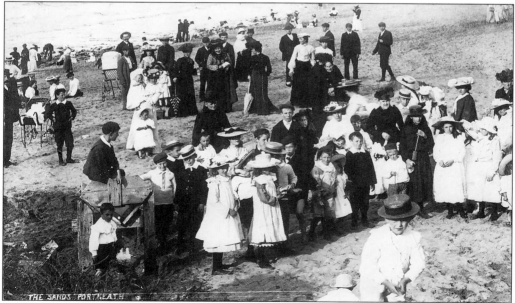

Members of Portreath Chapels enjoying their tea-treat on the beach.

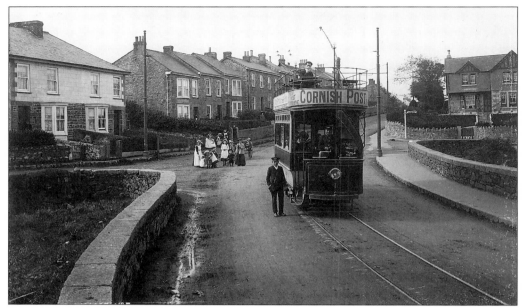
Tram No.4 at Rounding Walls Junction of Chariot Road.

What I have tried to show are the streets and shops, people and transport as they were in the early part of the century. No doubt we can all recall certain moments from the past, the annual tea-treat, the fair on Whit-Monday, Redruth Exhibition Show or perhaps the service at Gwennap Pit. Something, sometime, our own piece of nostalgia.

I hope that you get as much pleasure and enjoyment from looking through this book as I have had putting it together.

Paddy Bradley
Redruth
August 1995

One
Streets and Shops

To describe Redruth and its streets as one of the more attractive places to visit would be stretching ones imagination somewhat, yet it does have character, the type of character that is associated with a town steeped in industrial history. Wherever you go in Redruth some building or other can be linked to a famous person of days gone by, Murdoch, Trevithick and Watt to name but three.

Although the town centre has altered very little since the early 19th century, the population has obviously increased and more shops have appeared. We now have pedestrianisation in the lower part of Fore Street and yet there still remains the character.

Walk through the town, look up to the tops of the buildings and imagine what it must have been like in those days. Visit the places where those great engineers lived who brought recognition to the town and pride to its people.

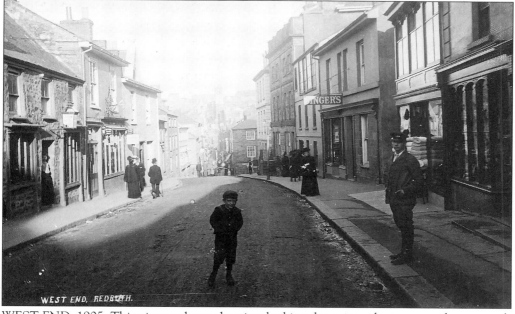

WEST END, REDRUTH.

WEST END, 1905. This picture shows the view looking down into the town on the approach from Camborne. Although this is not much different from today's view, some of the shop-fronts have changed. On the left John Beers shoe shop and Fauckners cycle shop were later replaced by Jones cycle shop which is now a local pasty making business. On the right Donnithornes Drapers (now Ann's Gowns) and Colemans, confectioners and agents for Singer Sewing Machines. Bank House and the original Police Station (now Arts and Graphics) were further down the road towards the town.

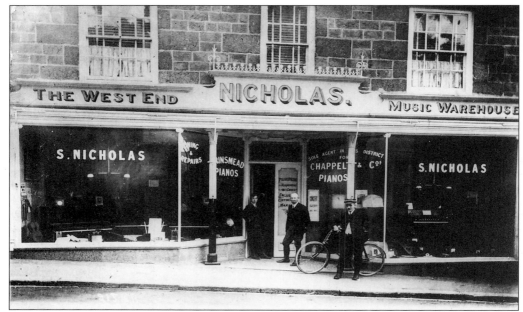

NICHOLAS c.1910. Stephen Nicholas, Musical Warehouse and Pianos, whose family was well connected in local musical circles. Charles, his son, was the leader of several choral groups. Remfrey Jarvis took over the shop, later on selling Hornby and Meccano products. Now it is Real Estates, estate agents.

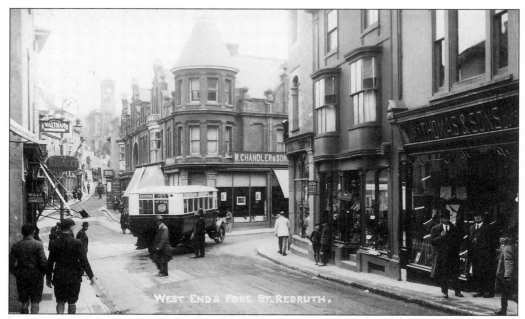

WEST END, 1930. An old Cornwall Motor Transport (CMT) bus coming from Camborne turns into Penryn Street on its way to the terminus by the Post Office in Alma Place. Thomas & Son, Mens Tailors and Outfitters is on the right, then Lawns Woolshop and Gammies the Chemist.

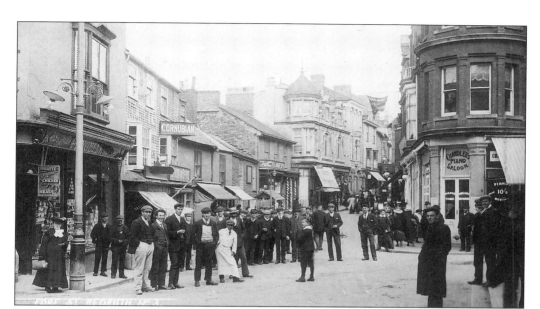

FORE STREET, 1907. Taken at the junction of West End, Penryn Street and Chapel Street. Pengellys grocers shop was a thriving business at the time but it was demolished in 1960 to make way for the road widening of Chapel Street. Also seen on the left is Nicholls barbers shop and the offices of the Cornubian Newspaper. The small houses that follow include the old Kings Head Inn, these latter houses were pulled down in 1935 to make way for the Regal Cinema. On the right is Chandlers Piano Saloon, also agents for various shipping lines, later this site was occupied by John Knights Furnishing Department, now Black Horse Agencies, estate agents.

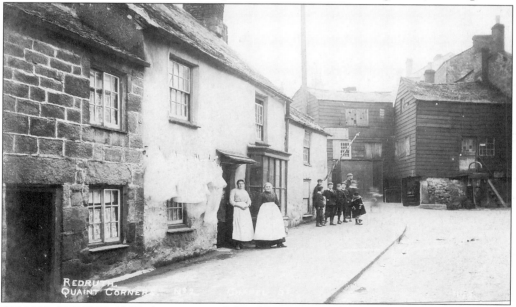

CHAPEL STREET, 1905. A rare view of the old cottages and Goodmans furniture workshop where there was also an old water wheel until 1913. The cottages seen here and Riverside Terrace (behind) were pulled down in 1935 to make way for the Regal Cinema and widening the entrance to the Cornish Meat & Provision Company.

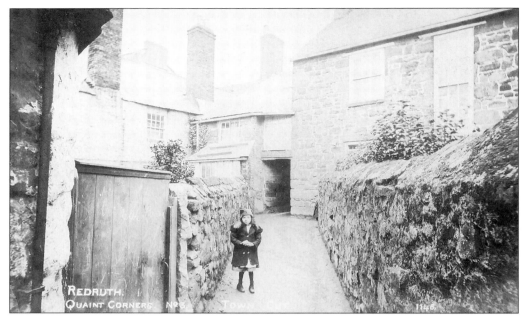

TOWN CUT, 1905. Although there is still a walkway beside the Regal Cinema this particular one has long gone, everything in the picture was demolished when the Regal Cinema was being built in 1935.

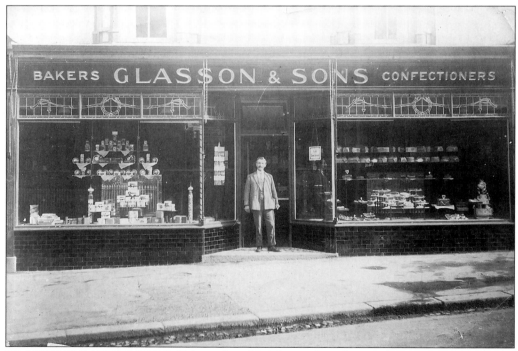

GLASSONS BAKERY SHOP. Taken when Mr Glasson (standing in doorway) first purchased and opened his bakery shop in 1925, prior to this the premises were used by Phillips & Stephens Cycle Shop. It is adjacent to the Rose Cottage Inn.

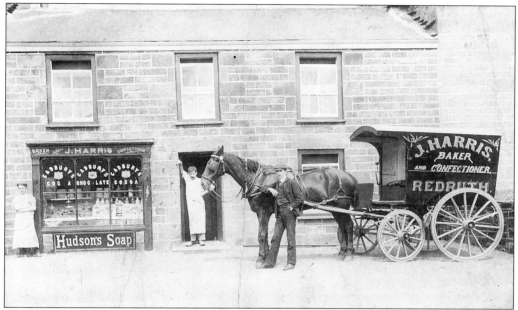

HARRIS BAKER & CONFECTIONER. Situated in Foundry Row just past the Police Station, this small family owned business carried on a thriving trade. The beautiful horse-drawn wagon would have travelled over large areas of the town and outlying countryside. The shop is now Bobs & Curls, hairdressing salon.

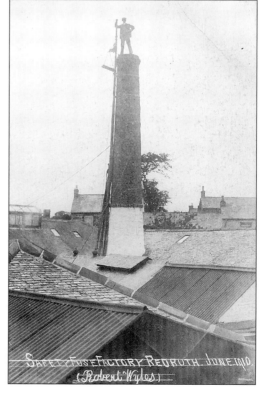

REDRUTH SAFETY FUSE FACTORY. The Fuse Factory itself was on the site of what is now the offices of Redruth Brewery Company, Chymbla House. The stack, part of which still stands, is having maintenance carried out by Mr Robert Wyles a local steeplejack.

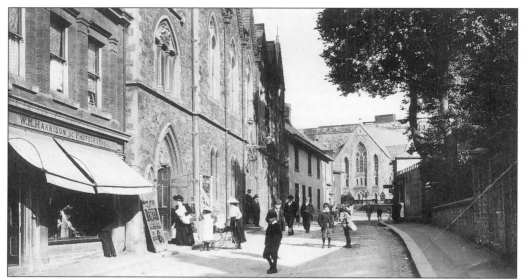

PENRYN STREET, 1905. The large building in the centre of the picture was known originally as the Druids Hall. It was built around 1859/60 for use as a meeting place for literary and scientific institutions. At the time this picture was taken an "American Bazaar" was taking place and was in its final week. In 1909 Redruth had its first cinema here, the Jenkins Picturedrome. It later became known as the Gem Cinema until it closed in 1959. After a short while it reopened as the Zodiac Bingo Hall, however, in 1980 one of Redruth's very large fires saw the final closure of what was a very fine building.

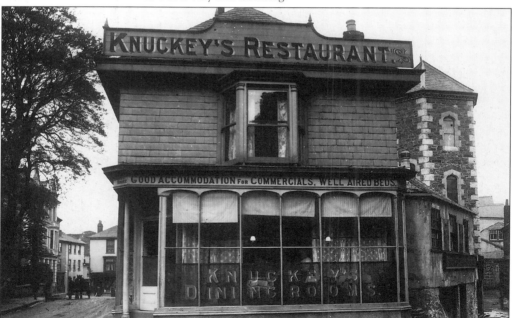

KNUCKEYS RESTAURANT, 1895. On the corner of Penryn Street and Cross Street and known once as Druids House, it has seen many changes over the years, the accommodation for travellers offers "well aired beds". Obviously a great comfort to those who stayed there. Now the site of the Hollies Hotel.

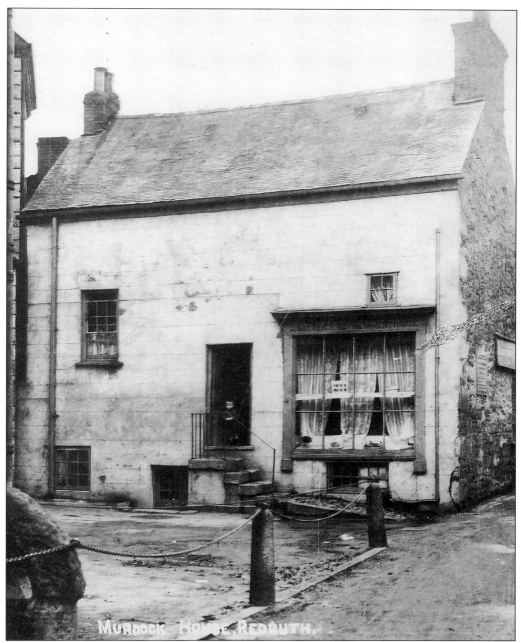

MURDOCH HOUSE. To people all over the world the name Murdoch will always be associated with gas. It was here in the early days (1792) that he discovered coal gas and used it as a form of lighting for the house and his office, which became the first building in the world to be lit by gas. It was also in Redruth that he made and tested the first locomotive in 1784, a small self-propelling engine which he took to Church Lane near St Euny one dark evening, in the process he almost frightened the life out of the local Rector. This photograph shows the building when it was Battens Refreshment House, taken just before the fire of 1920 which almost destroyed the building.

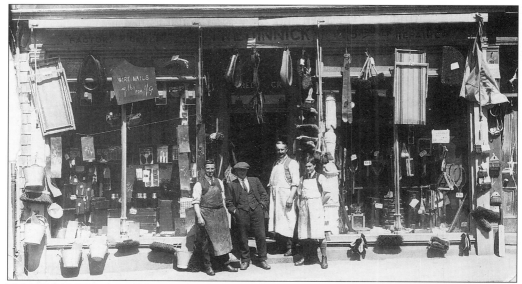

TREDINNICKS. A well-known local saddle and leather shop, renowned for the quality of the saddles, harnesses and other riding accessories. Originally the firm was established in Hayle around 1780 but moved to Redruth in the middle of the 19th century, the business closed in 1967.

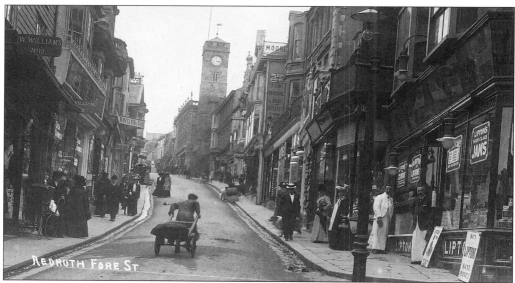

LOWER FORE STREET. This picture of lower Fore Street at the junction of Cross Street (Fish Cross) shows the various shops in the lower part of the town. Although there has not been a great deal of alteration to the actual street, apart from the present pedestrianisation, the shops have been altered. On the right Liptons advertising their own teas and jams (now a bakers shop and cafe), then Phillips Shoe Shop, later Miss Roskrows (still a shoe shop). These were followed by Smiths Boot & Shoe Shop (S.W.E.B), Wiltons Ironmongers, now Nicholas the Chemist. On the left there was Williams the butchers and Timothy Whites chemist and hardware shop, Kistlers jewellers shop followed by Michells, Redruth Clothing Company. These are now replaced by LoCost, a charity shop and a card shop.

EDWARDS, 1912. One of the many family-owned shops in the town, this particular one, a grocers, had every staple requirement. Note the sign for Bovril which was obviously a popular drink even in those days. They also had a shop on the opposite side of the road where they sold all types of best quality china.

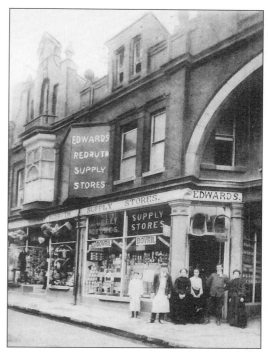

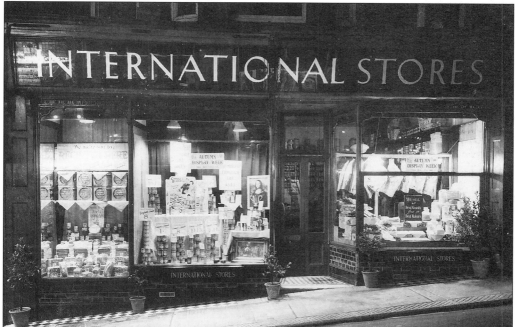

INTERNATIONAL STORES. One of the newer shops, this photograph was taken in 1950 when the town was getting ready for Shopping Week. How many can remember the quality of service from the manager (Mr Symes) and his staff? Obviously rationing was still in force as there is a request for people to 'register' – see left hand window. Note the various prices, slab fruit cake at 2/- to 2/8 per lb; tins of soup 8d, 10d and 1/3.

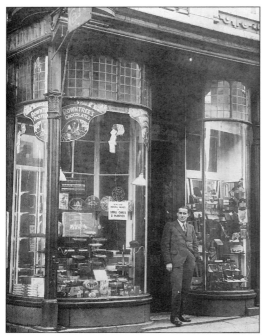

JOHNSONS. This little shop situated on the left hand side of Fore Street used to have curved windows, here Mr Johnson is standing in the entrance waiting for customers. Apart from selling anything to do with smoking – cigars, pipes and tobacco etc., he also sold fancy cakes, tins of biscuits and boxes of chocolates. There was also a small restaurant on the first floor; you had to go through the shop and up the stairs to have your afternoon tea.

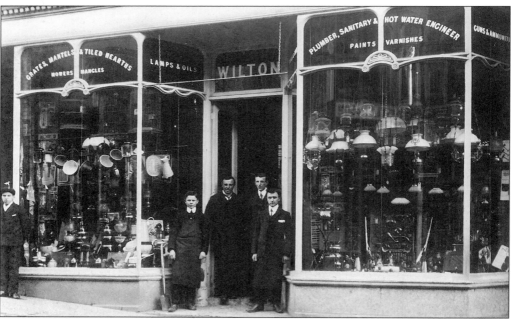

WILTONS. A type of shop that you do not often see these days, the old fashioned ironmongers and hardware business selling everything from a small nail to a large Cornish Range. It was another shop where courtesy and politeness were of paramount importance – "a chair to sit on whilst your order was being attended to". Remember the old paraffin lamps, enamelled pots and pans and numerous other goods that were sold by the four gentlemen in the doorway? From left to right : Mr Chappell, Mr Roberts, Mr Wilton and Mr Dyer. After 88 years of trading the business finally closed in 1968. Nicholas the chemist now occupies the site.

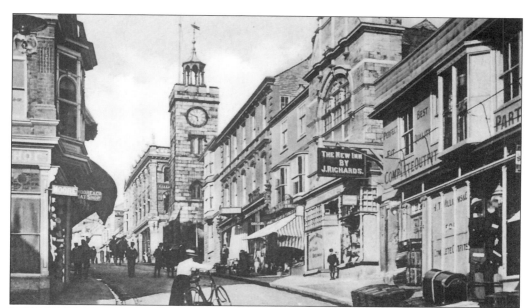

MIDDLE FORE STREET 1904.This and the following photograph show some of the changes that have taken place in Fore Street over the years. In the first picture you can see that H. T. Williams had two shops, the first for mens clothing and the second for ladies fashions. Through the alleyway between the shops was the New Inn public house. The biggest change, however, is in the Town Clock which in this view stands at fifty feet with a wooden top section.

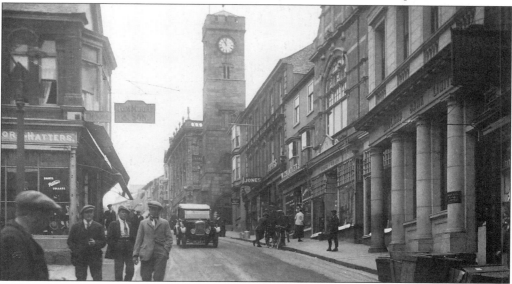

MIDDLE FORE STREET 1930. In this picture the changes are quite apparent. The bottom shop of H T Williams has been replaced by the Midland Bank, the public house has closed and both mens and ladies clothing are now in one building. Motor transport has replaced horse-drawn wagons. However, it is in the clock that changes are most evident. All the top section has been altered, an additional 20 feet has been added to the height and a new tower built above the changed clock faces. For installing these new workings and raising the stonework the total cost was almost £500.

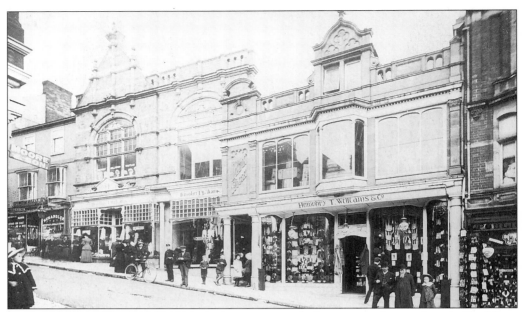

HUMPHREY T WILLIAMS 1910. A close-up view of what was an elegant shop and building, the left hand section still remains in the form of Clinton Cards. The ornate top is still in place and in the windows the words "Dresses, Milliners, Mantles" are fairly legible – signs of times long gone.

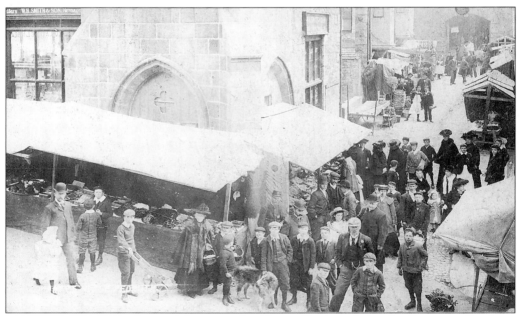

MARKET STRAND. Situated between the Town Clock and the De Dunstanville Arms (Fosters) this small cobbled thoroughfare led up to the Market entrance. The picture taken on Market Day shows stalls (standings) heavily laden with different produce. The stall prominent in the front belonged to the Hick family who made boiled sweets, remember the types – Clidgey, Nicies, Tom Trot, Bulls Eyes and many others?

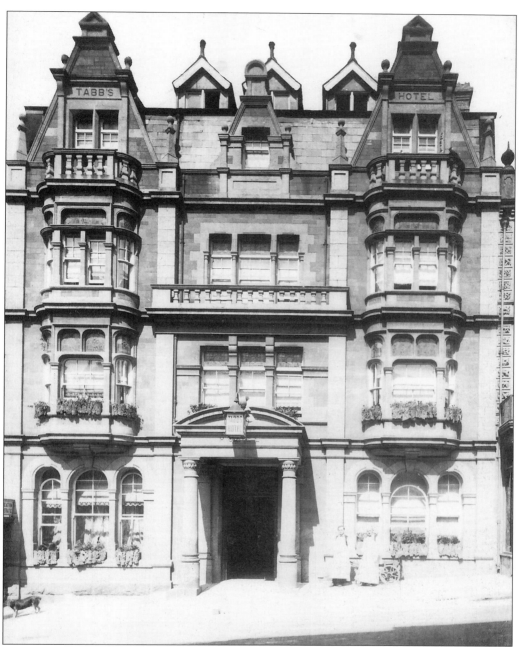

TABBS HOTEL. Situated in the middle of Fore Street this fine building is no longer standing, it was pulled down in 1970 to make way for a new Tesco Store. The original hotel, built in 1700 was, unfortunately, destroyed by fire in 1893. It was then rebuilt as seen here. As well as a hotel, local mine-owners used the premises to carry out what was known as "Ticketing", a process where tin and copper would be sold to the highest bidder. In 1880 this all moved to the Mining Exchange in Alma Place. During the 1939/45 war the hotel was used for many purposes such as a hostel and sick-bay. It was also used as a Red Shield Club for American Soldiers and by many other groups.

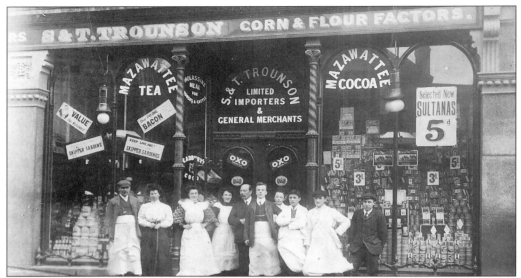

TROUNSONS. This was an old family business established in 1871, known as the "largest importers of saffron". It was a magnificent shop to go into and as one opened the door the smell of freshly ground coffee was all around. Note the products being advertised – sultanas 5d a lb (2p today), Skipper sardines, Mazawattee tea and coffee – heady days indeed. The two gentlemen in the centre of the picture are Mr Middleton on the left and Mr Pascoe on the right. This is now the site of Superdrug.

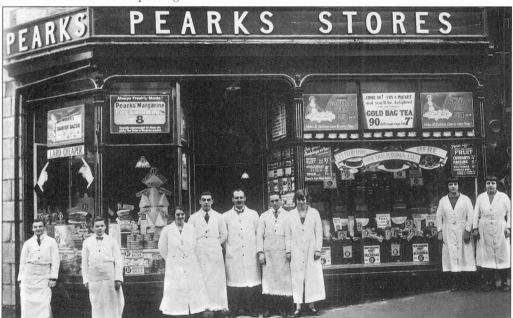

PEARKS - 1926. Located on the corner of Fore Street and Green Lane a branch of one of the large multiple stores that came to the town in the early part of the 1900s. See the eye-catching adverts – Gold Bag tea 90 cups for 7d (3p), freshly made margarine rolls at 8d per lb, sultanas 8d per lb. The two ladies on the right are the Shelton sisters. It is now a part of Boots the Chemist building.

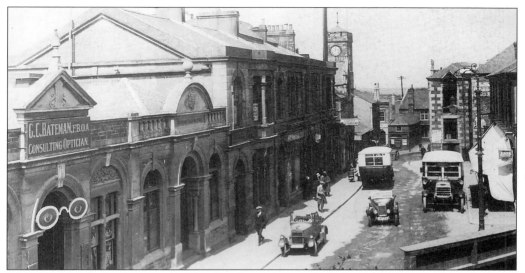

ALMA PLACE. At one time known as Jenkins Ope it was renamed after one of the battles of the Crimean War. A very busy street it contained the Post Office and the Mining Exchange as well as the Alma Hotel, Coffee Tavern and Trounsons Warehouse, plus a few other businesses. It was also the terminus for the C.M.T. bus routes for Truro, Camborne and Falmouth. The Mining Exchange, seen on the left, was built in 1880 and took over all the tin and copper ticketing from Tabbs Hotel, it is now used by Age Concern. Further down was the old Post Office and Telegraph Office, there until it was moved to its new site in Fore Street in 1957/58. The Ministry of Agriculture and Fisheries took over the building after the move and remained there until the whole of the building was gutted by fire in September 1982 – it remains in that state at present. The next building was the Coffee Tavern built in 1879, it had a Temperance Hall upstairs and a restaurant (Rowes). The Lamb and Flag was below, now a fish and chip shop.

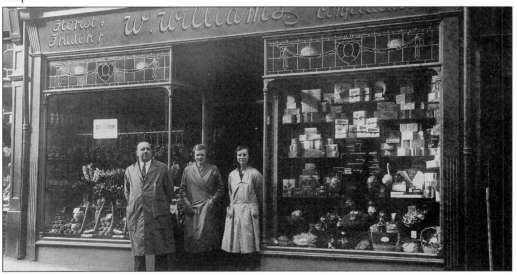

WILLIAMS. A beautiful fruit, vegetable and confectioners shop in Alma Place near Fore Street next to Jennings Saddlers. Here Mr Williams and his staff, Phyllis Abrahams and Moira Henwood pose for the photographer. Flair Fashions occupies the site now.

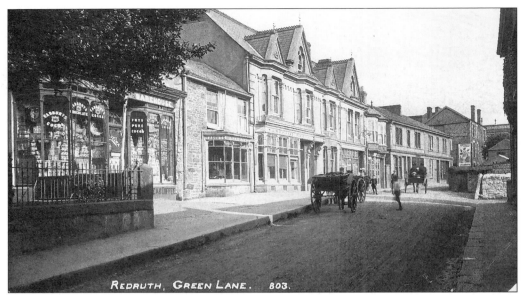

REDRUTH, GREEN LANE. 803.

GREEN LANE. Looking at this street today it does not appear to have altered a great deal except the first shop, Foulkes grocers, which has now been completely demolished and is a small car park. Williams, poulterer is now Collins fish and chip shop and Rickard the butchers is now empty. All the other businesses, Collins tobacconist, Goldsworthy barber and Edgar Rowe's Removals have all stopped trading.

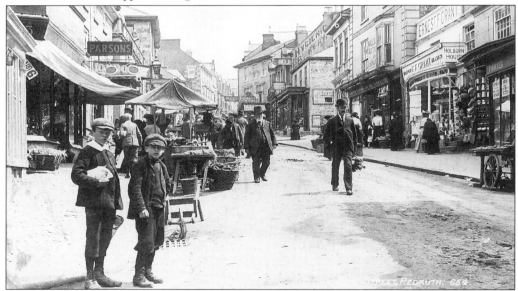

...REET REDRUTH. 654.

FORE STREET. Taken on a market day around 1907, this photograph shows what a busy place it was with stalls lining the street and shops displaying their wares. The shops, and in most cases their fronts, have been altered quite considerably since these early days. Ernest Grant and Burridge were combined into Whittakers, now Cockings Ladies Fashions and Wales was altered slightly and became Preston Johns, now Tregonnings furniture shop. Where the gap is on the right was Jacks Splatt and is now the site of the Post Office. On the left Star Supplies and Parsons (Cornelius) the jeweller are now Olivers book and record shop.

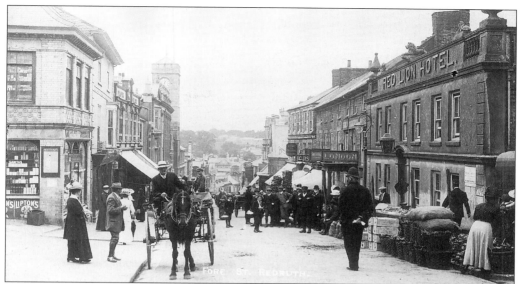

FORE STREET. This view is from a little further up Fore Street but this time looking down. Again it is market day with the local policeman strolling around keeping his eye on things, no doubt there was a clip around the ear for any youngster misbehaving. The alterations to the buildings on the left have taken place, note Whittakers new shop front. On the right the Red Lion Hotel (where I spent my early childhood) with the old stone balustrade and lions on the top. I remember a Mr Bray from Troon having a fruit and vegetable stall in the car park of the hotel.

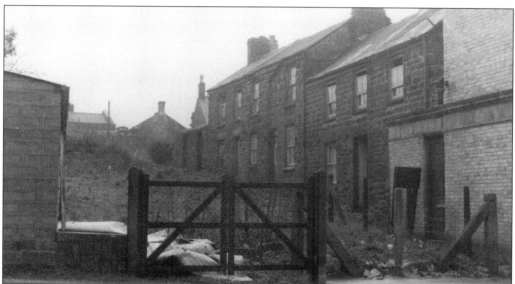

JACKS SPLATT. Taken during the early 1950s prior to work being done on the new Post Office. There are not many photographs of this view of Jacks Splatt. At times the area was used to hold part of the Whitsun Fair (late 1800s) whilst during the 1939-45 war an emergency water tank and two air raid shelters were built at the top end. The old cottages on the right were all inhabited at the time. Mr James a blind man and his family lived in the first one, in the second were evacuees from London called King and the third was the home of the Pearce family. The two openings past the last house were the entrances to the outside toilets.

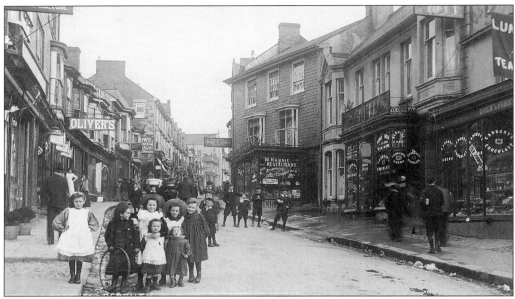

FORE STREET, 1905. For some reason not many photographs are available looking up to the top end of Fore Street, this one shows the view from outside the Red Lion to the junction of Shoot Row. Over the years this part of the road has seen many changes. Gone are the lovely ornate shop fronts with their enticing adverts. On the left was Gordons draper stores with the Temperance Hotel upstairs, then another part of Olivers Shoe shop, followed by Maunds (Lobbs) mens clothing shop. These have been replaced by Bartles meat shop, Eastmans (now closed) and The Wool Basket. On the right Drews confectioners and tea room later F.T. Balls grocer, with Snells Bakery next door followed by Harris, later Williams, bakers and restaurant. The entrance to the Post Office is now the first building with a wines and spirit shop next, the gas showrooms have now closed and a building society occupies the last site.

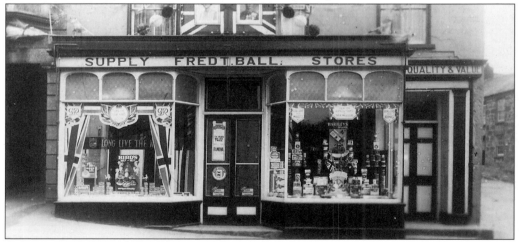

FRED T. BALL. Another of the many grocers shops in the town. This was on the left of Jacks Splatt where the entrance to the Post Office is now, at one time this was the site of Moody the photographer, father of Fanny Moody the "Cornish Nightingale". The picture, taken in 1937, shows that the Coronation was being celebrated whilst in the window an advert for the Regal Cinema shows that "The Man Who Lived Twice" and "Ramona" were being shown.

SNELLS. This was a long established bakers shop and was on the right going up Fore Street next to Fred Ball. Mr Snell is seen standing in the doorway looking pleased with himself. All the baking was done on site; the ovens can still be seen today at the back. Note the lovely adverts – own made gingerbreads, macaroons, Xmas puddings.

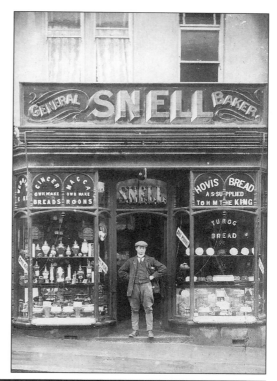

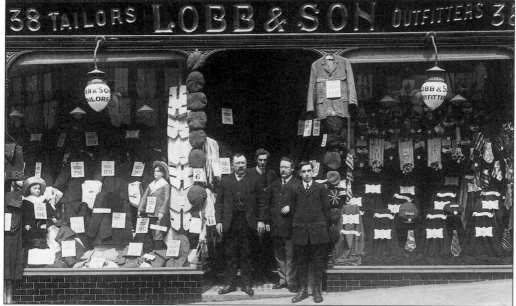

LOBB & SON. Mr Lobb and his staff posing in the doorway of his shop in the upper part of Fore Street. Every type of mens and boys clothing could be had here. Window dressing must have taken quite a time. See the little boy's velvet suit at 13/6 (67 Qw p) whilst men's suits and waistcoats range from 25/6 (127 Qw p) to 3/11 (20p), and shirts were available at 3/6 (17 Q w p). Oh what glorious days! Note the beautiful gas lamps hanging down.

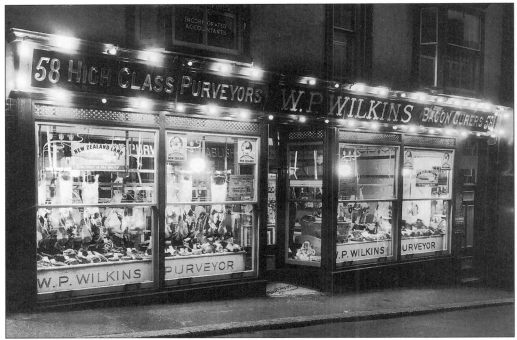

WILKINS. A family butcher of the highest quality, the shop has been laid out for the Redruth Shopping Week display of 1955. A fine selection of lamb can be seen in the left hand window.

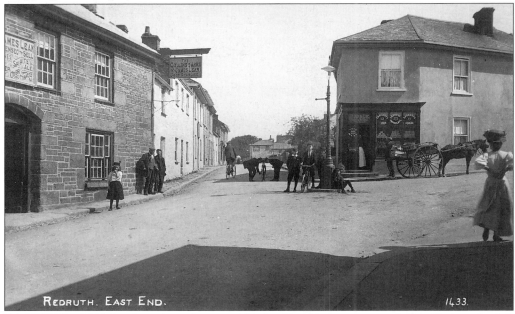

EAST END - 1910. Looking from the top of Higher Fore Street up towards East End on the left and St Day Road on the right, this was known as Buddles Corner. On the left is the Collins Arms home of the Lean family since 1786, named after the Rector of Redruth the Reverend Collins (1734-1775). The old gas lamp standing in the centre of the road was supposedly removed to allow motor vehicles to go more easily up through St Day Road.

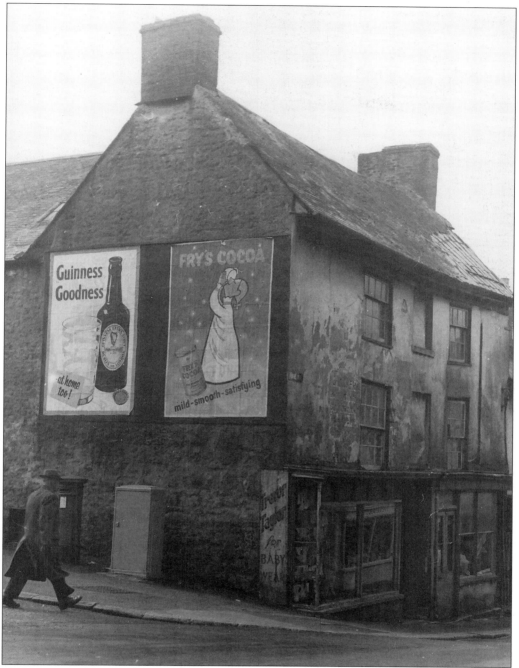

TAYLORS. The last building on the right as you went up through Fore Street, it specialised in baby wear and childrens clothes. Just below Taylors was Bert Roberts fish & chip shop whilst around to the left would have been some steps leading up to Sam Tucker's barber shop. As you can see the house is not in too good a state of repair and it was no surprise when it was pulled down in 1970. There is a small triangle between the top windows showing a date of 1711, identifying it as one of the oldest houses in the town.

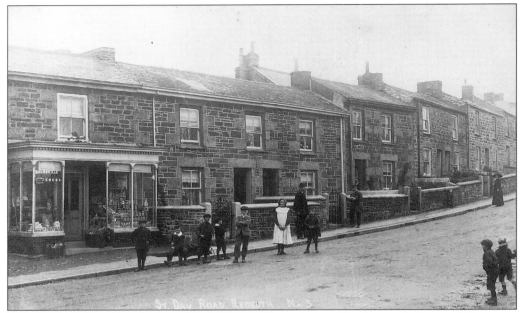

ST DAY ROAD. Taken around 1905 this view shows the road leading to St Day and Gwennap Pit. The houses have not altered much but the grocers shop no longer exists. Directly opposite this row of houses was the terminus of the old Redruth and Chacewater railway, granite sleeper blocks can still be seen there today.

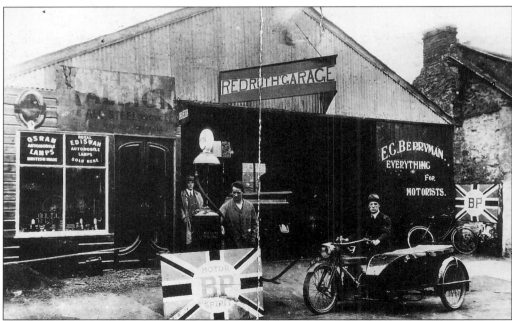

BERRYMANS GARAGE. One of the earlier garages in the town, it was located in East End on what used to be Mewtons butchers shop and the old Jehovah Witness Hall, now gone to be replaced by two private dwellings. Transport has certainly changed, see the old motor cycle and sidecar (possibly a Douglas), receiving petrol at around 1/- (5p) a gallon.

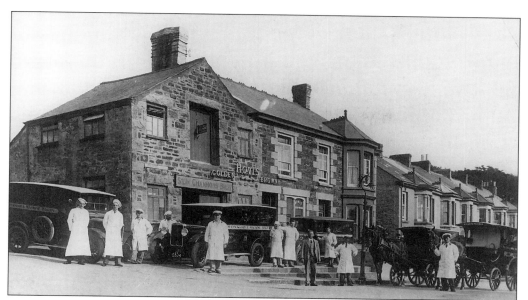

CHANNONS BAKERY. A sign of the changing times? From the old horse drawn bakers wagon to the more modern motor van. A marvellous view showing Channons Steam Bakery at Sea View Terrace with the staff assembled. There is still a bakery, Berrymans, here today.

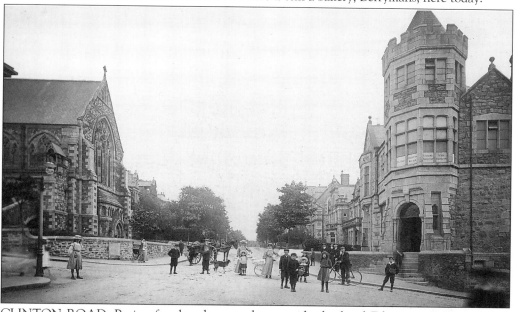

CLINTON ROAD. Posing for the photographer outside the local Education Offices and St Andrews Church at the junction of Heanton Terrace and Treruffe Hill with Clinton Road in the background. Not greatly altered since the photograph was taken in 1907, both buildings have recently celebrated their centenaries, the church in 1983 and the Education Offices/Library this year 1995. Do you remember Mr Hayman as the Education Officer later to become the local M.P.? The whole of the building now consists of the Public Library on the ground level whilst upstairs is the Cornish Local Studies Library, a most valuable asset, preserving Cornish history.

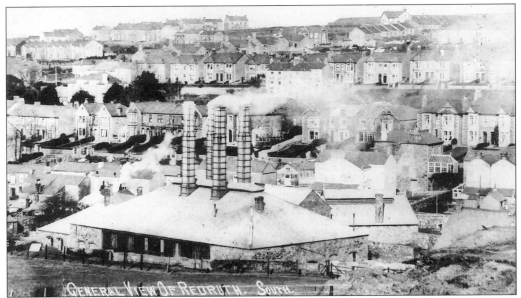

SOUTHGATE TURNPIKE. Approaching Redruth from the Falmouth and Helston directions around 1910, this imposing building would catch your eye. The Redruth Smelting Works, started in 1862, was used to smelt or whiten the tin after it had been extracted, and in 1923. It was used at one time by the Local Council as a storeyard and is now occupied by a local builder. Nearby is the well known Morrish's fish & chip shop.

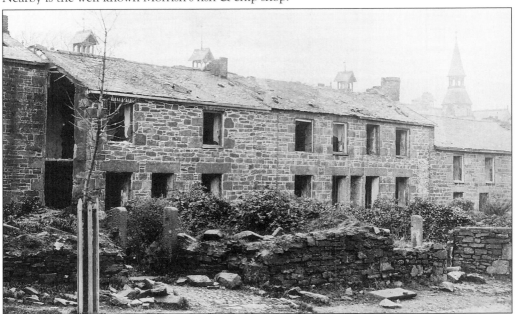

FALMOUTH ROAD. These old cottages in front of Trewirgie School were pulled down in 1914 to allow for the development of the girls netball courts and Mr Hensley's woodwork building. How many old Trewirgie "Water Rats" remember those early days at the school. Recent reunions of former pupils show how much interest there was. Do you remember the teachers? (See later photographs of some of them).

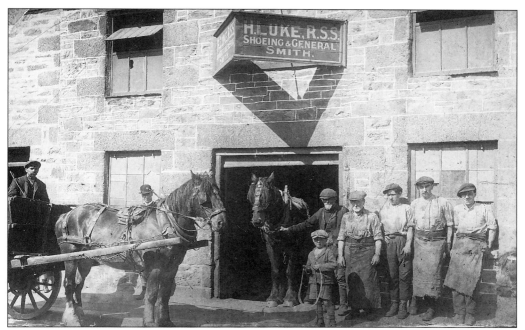

LUKES - BLACKSMITH. As you passed Trewirgie School, going towards the railway viaduct, from an open doorway on the right could be heard the sound of hammer on metal. This was the sound of Mr Henry Luke, blacksmith and his staff making horse shoes. Do you remember looking in through this open door and seeing the forges with their fires burning fiercely and the smell of the horses hooves as the new shoes were applied?

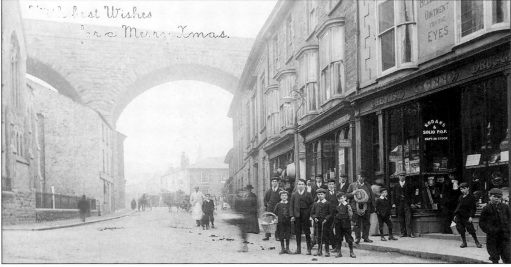

PENRYN STREET. Approaching the bottom of Fore Street from the Falmouth Road direction, one can see the magnificent granite viaduct of the G.W.R. main line to Penzance. The building on the left was the earliest theatre for live performances in the town, part of which was pulled down to enable the Baptist Chapel to be built. On the right, after the three shops of Mr Gee, chemist, Mr Martin, newsagent and one other, came the old Redruth Court House built in 1850 by Robert Blee, which is now the Gentlemans Club.

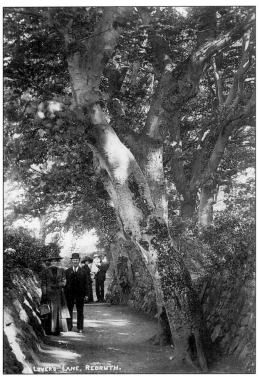

LOVERS LANE. No doubt many will have happy memories of this little lane, linking Trewirgie Road with Church Lane. It bordered on the property of Mr Hamilton Jenkin and was a well known courting spot.

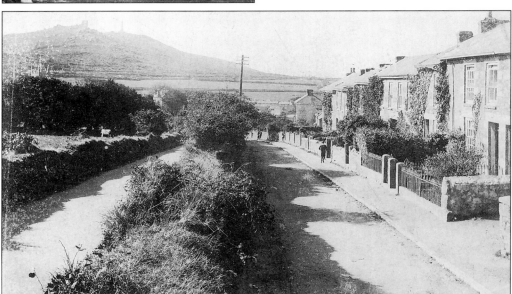

TREVINGIE TERRACE. Looking down this road the prominent hill of Carn Brea dominates the sky line, the lane on the left is the continuation of Church Lane, the route from the town to the Parish Church of St Euny. It was in this lane in 1784 Richard Murdoch tested out his steam locomotive, frightening the life out of the local Rector. The hedge dividing the two roads has long been removed down as far as the cemetery and a new bungalow estate has been built in the fields on the left.

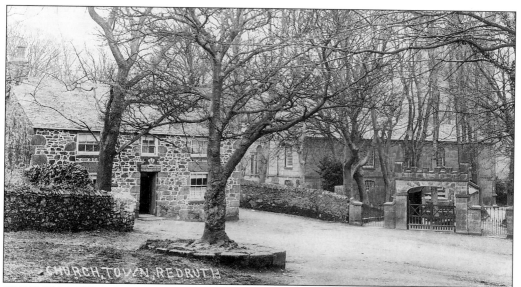

CHURCHTOWN. Opposites attract, so they say. Here we have the Parish Church of St Euny showing the lychgate and on the left the Plume of Feathers, a well known local hostelry which has been closed for some considerable time.

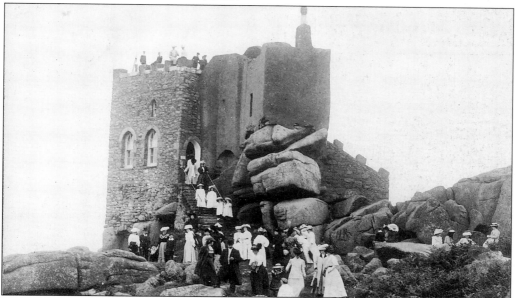

CARN BREA, THE CASTLE. Dominating the skyline for miles around this granite hill forms a part of the spine of Cornwall standing almost 750 feet above sea level. It has a history dating back to the time of the Ancient Druids and Romans. Throughout the ages there have been archaeological finds of great importance and stories and tales abound of this fascinating place. Built upon a large granite rock the early history of the castle is virtually unknown although dates of 1478 and 1754 have been mentioned. It has been said that at one time it was used as a chapel for the Bassett family, it has also been used as a dwelling place and is now a restaurant. The view from the roof is spectacular, Trevose to the north, the clay district to the east, Trencrom and Helston to the south and St Ives and beyond to the west. It is well worth a visit.

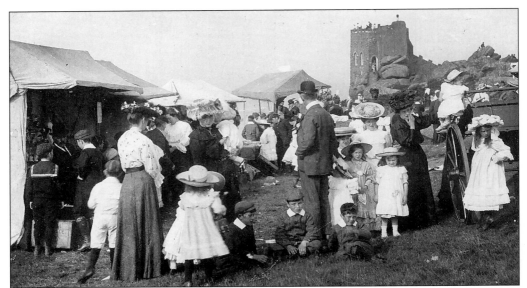

CARN BREA. Over the years many local chapels spent their "Tea Treat" days on the Carn. Saffron buns and tea, plus tables, chairs etc., were carried to the appropriate space provided by enthusiastic members of the congregation. Here we see in some detail what efforts were made to ensure the event was a success – see how everyone is dressed up in their Sunday best.

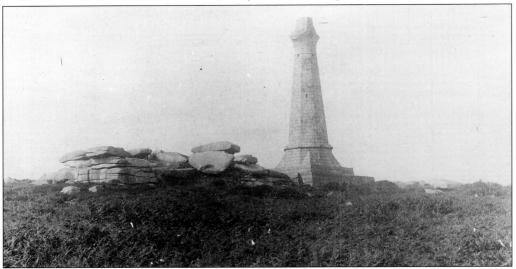

CARN BREA, THE MONUMENT. Standing some ninety feet high in the middle of the Carn, this large granite pillar was erected by public subscription to the memory of Francis Lord De Dunstanville. The foundation stone was laid in 1836 and when dedicated it was reported that "a large gathering of some 30,000 people were present". There used to be a wooden staircase on the inside but with the passage of time this has rotted away. Those who have taken the opportunity to visit this historic site have many marvellous memories of the views which stretch over the industrial heart of Cornwall. Sit on the rocks and see where the old tin mines used to be, East Pool, Crofty, Dolcoath and many more, imagine the miners coming up from underground. Those of you who have not made the journey to the top do not know what you have missed.

Two
Characters and Groups

Each and every town has its own particular characters, some of them are legendary – Redruth is no exception. This section deals with some individuals and groups. I am sure that you will all have your own favourite stories that could be added to these.

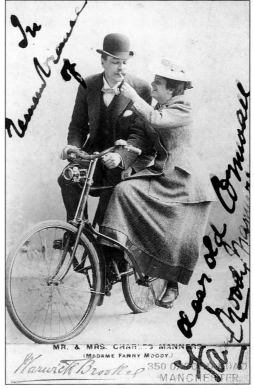

FANNY MOODY. The "Cornish Nightingale" born in her father's photographers shop in Fore Street, corner of Jacks Splatt in 1866. She attended Mr and Mrs Chellews High School for Girls and was later taken under the wing of Lady Bassett who paid for her singing lessons. After completing her training she joined the famous Carl Rosa Opera Company where she met and married Mr Charles Manners. She died in Dundrin, Co. Dublin in July 1945.

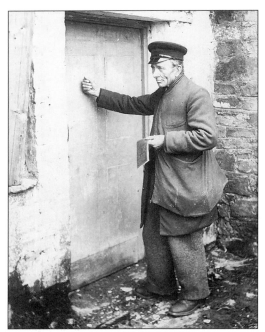 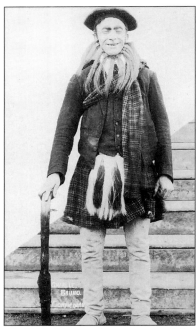

Top, left: TOM BARNEY WINKS. Also known as Tom Enny Tozer, he used to go around the town selling Doidges Almanacs. Top, right: CHARLIE BRUNO. One of the very well-known clowns/comedians who used to travel around Cornwall and Devon with Anderton and Rowlands Fairs.

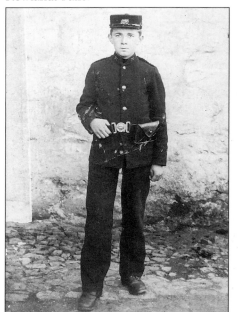 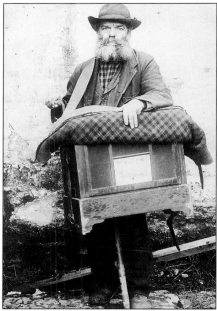

Bottom, left: MR WEBB. One of the local telegram boys at Redruth Post Office. Bottom, right: ORGAN JOE. It is thought that he came from the Plymouth area. Whenever any of the Fairs were in town he would arrive at Hicks in Higher Fore Street and sleep in the stables. He would travel around playing this barrel organ and no doubt make a reasonable living.

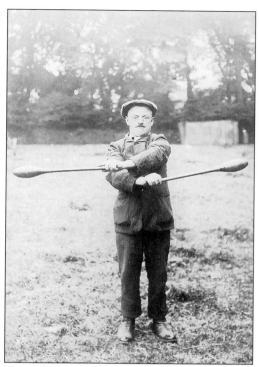

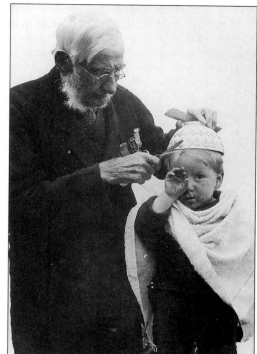

Top, left: FREDDIE SNELL. How many can remember Freddie Snell? Perhaps like me you remember him having lost his sight. What about his song and dance routine? Drop some money in his tin and he would sing various songs and do a little jig. One tune I remember was "Ain't no sense sitting on the fence all by yourself in the moonlight."

Top, right: THE ORIGINAL BASIN CUT. This elderly gentleman is a Mr Howard of the Illogan area. The picture was taken in 1905 when he was aged 83. As you can see he has medals fixed to his coat, these were awarded during the Crimean War.

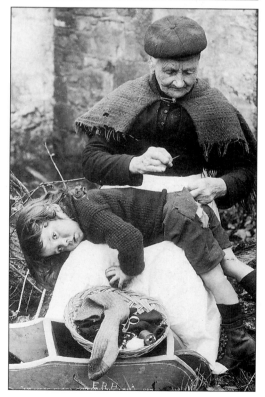

PATCHES. Although Grandma's hands look full of arthritis, she seems to have things under control. Perhaps the young boy had been up on the "sliding rock" on Carn Brea.

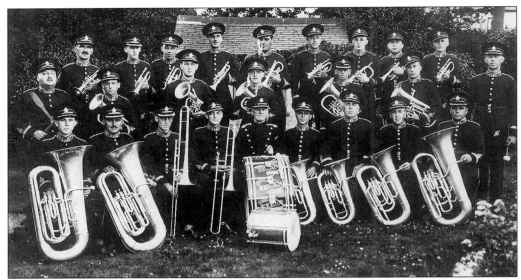

REDRUTH BAND - 1931. The band was formed in 1905 and has performed all over the County with great distinction. It was the very first band to perform live for the B.B.C. back in 1936 at Bodmin. In 1935 at Falmouth they won the Open Section contest for the first time and at the National Band Championships at Alexandra Palace they came third in Section 3, a notable achievement. Back row, left to right: Joe Reynolds, Clifford Harris, Otto Rhilmann, Stanley Coombes, Jack Williams, Ivor Watts, Harry Eddy, Stanley Parsons, Telfor Kent, Dick Bray. Middle row: Sam Chegwidden, ? Gilbert, George Martin, Walter Williams, ? Gilbert, Fred Bawden. Front row: George Robinson, Dick Penaluna, Norman Reynolds, Ivor Hosking, Mr Charles Baker (Conductor), Ernie Pearce, Bill Tremayne, Alfie Opie, ? Parkyn.

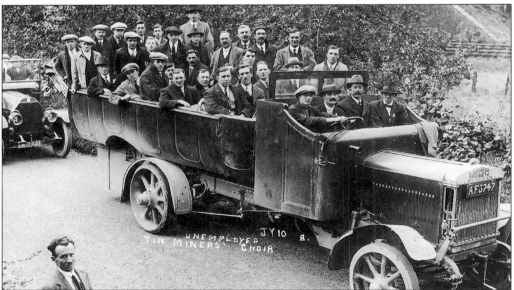

UNEMPLOYED TIN MINERS CHOIR. The choir was formed to raise money for the distressed miners and their families when the great mines started to close down. Thousands were put out of work and families faced great hardships. Many of the choir were themselves miners.

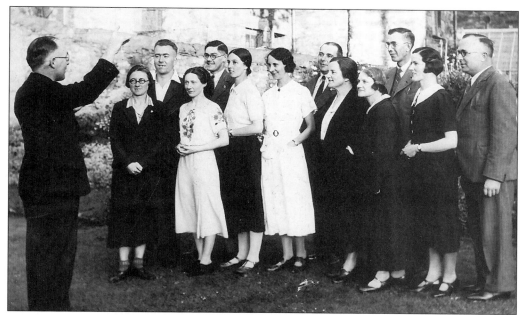

REDRUTH MADRIGAL SINGERS 1938. Music has played a great part in the lives of many Redruth families, singing it seemed was a part of their inheritance. This was one of the many groups that performed around the district under the guidance of Mr Charles Nicholas (left). The gentleman on the left, back row, Mr Leslie Millington, was also a conductor and organist of great skill. Back row, left to right: Leslie Millington, Hugh Pengelly, Edgar Rowe, Everitt Treneer, Jack Hill. Front row: Lottie Munday, P. Kneebone, Joy Millington, O. Trethowan, Clarice Visick, Gertrude Munday, R. Philps.

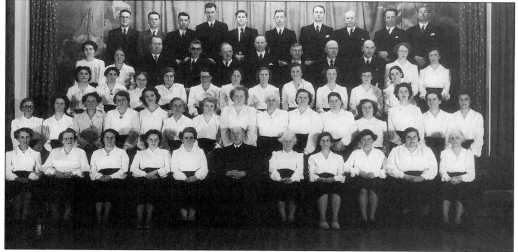

REDRUTH CHORAL SOCIETY. Another of the musical groups that came under the guidance of Mr Charles Nicholas, this one, however, has a long and proud history. Formed over 125 years ago, one of its many noticeable successes was in 1951 when they won through numerous qualifying rounds to enable them to sing at the Festival of Britain in Battersea Park. Well-known members included Jim Ham, Leslie Thomas, Leslie Millington, Marie Trevithick, Marjorie Collins, Joy Millington and Flo Saunders.

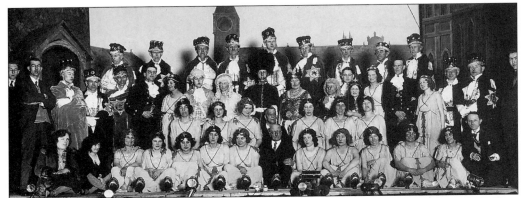

REDRUTH OPERATIC SOCIETY. The cast of the Society are seen after performing Gilbert & Sullivan's *Iolanthe* in 1931. Formed in 1909 when its first production was *H.M.S. Pinafore*, the Society has given many notable shows in its time. Many of the town's leading figures took active parts, Phyllis Tredinnick, Arthur Hendy, Mabel Williams, Joy and Leslie Millington and the conductor Mr Henry Dennis. The Society's first productions were performed in the old Druids Hall (Gem Cinema) but they moved to the more spacious Regal Cinema after 1935.

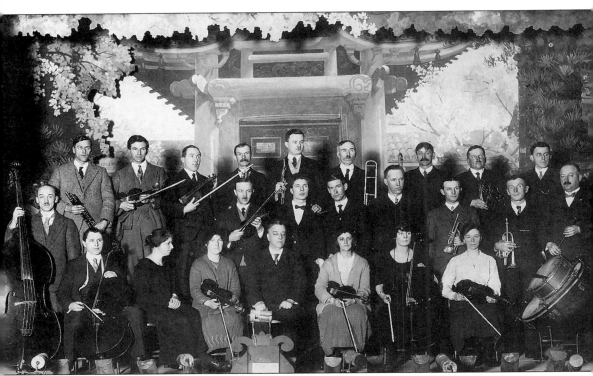

THE ORCHESTRA. Every musical production needed an orchestra and the Operatic Society was no exception. Here the members of the orchestra are assembled before the start of *The Mikado* in 1923. Back row, left to right: H. Oates, L. Hancock, C. Nicholas, H. Rogers, C. Pengelly, H. Northey, R. Jenkin, T. Venton, W. Richards. Centre row: N. Trevarthen, P. Rowe, D. Broad, J. Pengelly, P. Collins, J. Knight, S. Chegwidden. Front row: L. Opie, Miss Carling, Mrs L. Hancock, Mr H. Dennis, Miss Rigby, Miss Broad, Miss Climas.

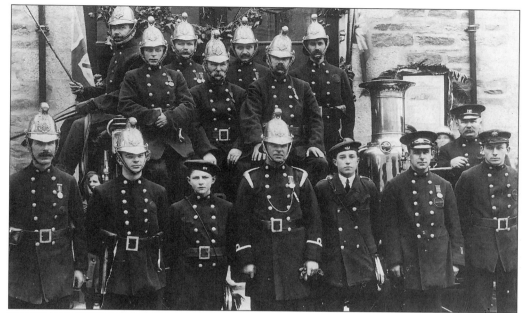

REDRUTH FIRE BRIGADE. Members of the local fire brigade ready for inspection outside their headquarters in Penryn Street. The engine is a Merryweather steam-operated and hand-pumped. Note the beautiful brass helmets. Back row, left to right: Bob Clinch (Driver), Jimmy Haley, Dick Truran, "Kissy Da" Nicholls, Dicky Oates, Jack Duncan, Ike Wallace. Front row: Willy Burns, Willy Olds, Frank Williams (1st Bugler), Bert Dallimore (Captain), Tom Lidgey (2nd Bugler), Willie Lanyon, Percy Trethowan, Sammy Trevena.

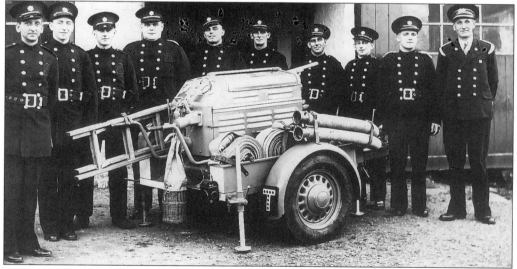

THE AUXILIARY FIRE BRIGADE (A.F.S.). Times have changed since the previous picture of the Fire Service, gone are the beautiful brass helmets and the horse-drawn Merryweather engine. Taken during the war, around 1940-41, outside Lanyons Garage in Falmouth Road, this shows one of the new trailer mounted pumps that were pulled by motor vehicles. Left to right: Joe Parkyn, Albert Symons, Fred Thomas, Francis Johns, -?-, Henry Stephens, Tommy Harris, Ken Gray, 'Art' Pethick (Captain).

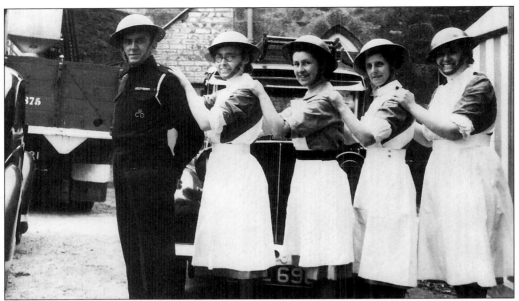

A FIRST AID GROUP. Remember the wartime period? Away from all the bombing we felt relatively safe in this part of the country, however, we did not escape completely. A lone German bomber who was probably lost, left his mark on the town, to be more precise the railway station. One person was killed at the station although six in total died during the raid, and several others were injured. They would have been given first aid treatment by volunteers such as these shown here. The picture was taken at the rear of the Wesley Chapel. Left to right: Mr Harold Kernick, Miss F. Paul, Miss F. Thomas, Mrs Trenter, Miss M. Jenkins.

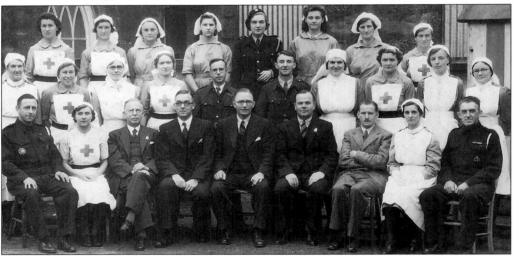

A RESCUE GROUP. Taken a little later, this group of volunteers consists of doctors and officials of the Red Cross, St Johns Ambulance, Civil Defence and Air Raid Precautions, again taken at the rear of Wesley Chapel. Back row, left to right: -?-, -?-, Mrs Viv Jeffrey, -?-, -?-, -?-, Miss Olive Tippett, Olive May. Middle row: Mrs E. J. Mitchell, -?-, Miss F. Paul, Miss M. Higgins, Mr Chas Angove, Mr Les Pappin, Miss M. Jenkin, Miss Patience Richards, Miss G. King, Miss Chris Julian. Front row: Mr Fred Polkinghorne, -?-, Mr A. Gee, Mr Willie Bishop, Dr MacDonald, Mr R. Blamey, -?-, Mrs Trenter, Mr H. Kernick.

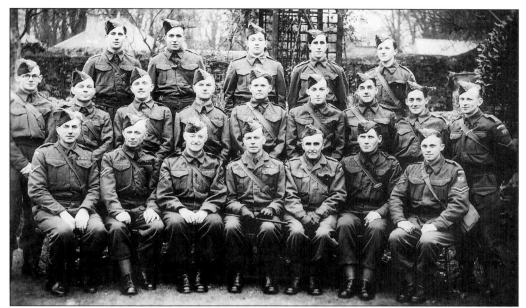

HOME GUARD. Or as today's television viewers would call them "Dads Army", one of the many groups/platoons that were formed and stationed in and around the Redruth district. This particular group picture was taken in the grounds of the "Elms", the home of the Trounson family. Back row, left to right: -?-, -?-, -?-, Don Langdon, -?-. Middle row: Ken Eva, Leslie Gilbert, Howard Glasson "Jelland" Thomas, Jack Trounson, Elijah Durrant, -?-, Willie Glasson, -?-. Front row: -?-, -?-, Frank Hayman, Mr Williamson, -?-, Howard Borlase, Bert Pryor.

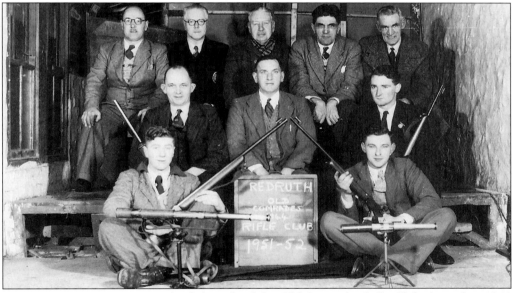

REDRUTH RIFLE CLUB. Redruth branch of the Old Comrades Rifle Club, formed in 1944 used to hold their meetings in the range beside the Old Drill Hall now the Community Centre. Back row, left to right: Walter Tredinnick, Mr Godber, Bernard Smith, 'Tino' Martin, Mr Stokes. Middle row: Mr Johnston, Jack Floyd, Donovan Wilkins. Front row: Donald Congden, Trevor Martin.

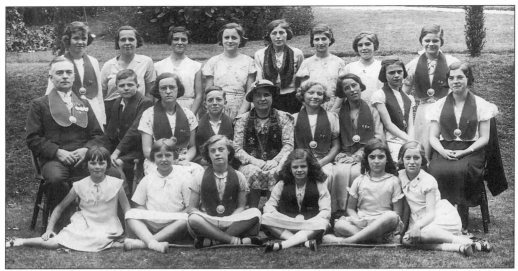

INDEPENDENT ORDER OF GOOD TEMPLARS (I.O.G.T.). Members of the local branch of the I.O.G.T. taken in the back garden of the "Elms", this was the Junior Section of a group of temperance people devoted to total abstinence. Back row, left to right: Pearl Jeffrey, Audrey Burrows, Ivy Broad, Marion Stevens, Mrs Small, Phyllis Stevens, -?-, Miss Foss. Middle row: Mr Nicholls, Jim Pearce, Pearl Nicholls, Garfield Pearce, Mrs Nicholls, Winnie Stevens, Nellie Johns, -?-, -?-. Front row: Joan Tonkin, -?-, -?-, Miss Foss, Jean Matthews, Mary Johns.

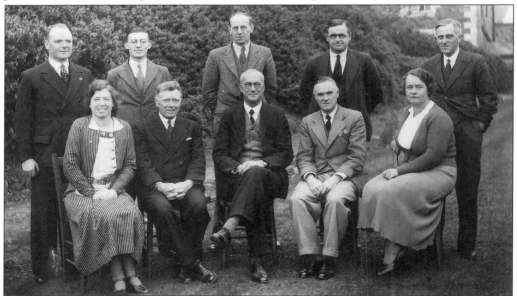

TREWIRGIE BOYS SCHOOL TEACHERS. No doubt many will have fond memories of their early school days, the good and the bad times, friendships made and friends now gone, and the teachers that did their best to give us the groundwork for a good education. Trewirgie was blessed with many such people and no doubt some of you will remember these here. Back row, left to right: Clifton Pellow (School Caretaker), Mr Owen, Mr Harold Hensley, Mr 'Dad' Thomas, Mr Hugh Downing. Front row: Miss Hunt, Mr Harris, Mr W. E. Shiers (Headmaster), Mr 'Jimmer' Phillips, Miss Blamey.

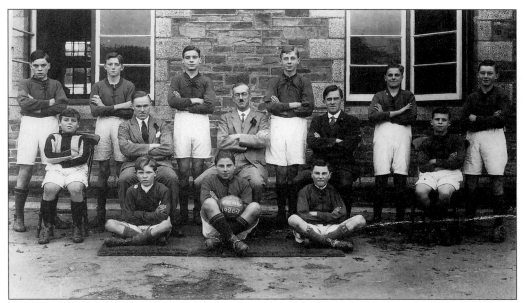

TREWIRGIE BOYS SCHOOL FOOTBALL TEAM 1926-27. Trewirgie was renowned for its sporting prowess both in football and rugby, producing several top class players who achieved success at schoolboy, club, county and international level several of whom can be seen in the next two photos. Back row, left to right: G. Robbins, G. Ferrycombe, S. Partridge, M. Wilson, R. Lenton, R. Matthews. Middle row: F. Glasson, Mr Phillips, Mr Shiers, Mr Downing, T. Harry. Front row: G. Woolcock, F. Bone, W. J. Harry.

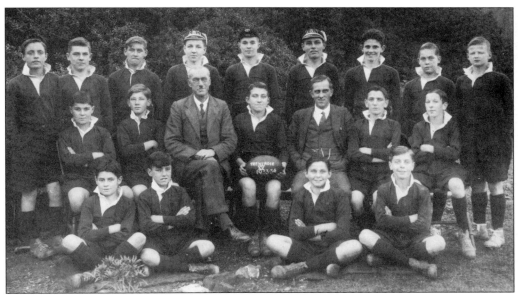

TREWIRGIE BOYS RUGBY TEAM 1933-34. Back row, left to right: Jack Stafford, Don Robbins, Leslie Faull, Don Scoble, Frank Partridge, Bernard Woods, Willie Knuckey, Peter Finch, Leonard Semmens. Middle row: Harry Glasson, Louvain Nicholls, Mr. W. E. Shiers, Jack Johns, Mr H. Downing, Percy Rule, Barnard Scoble. Front row: Leonard Goldsworthy, Frank Bray, Tony Bidgood, Jack Hicks.

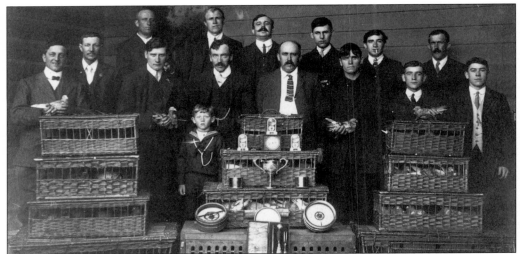

REDRUTH PIGEON CLUB, 1910. A very popular pastime in these early days was the breeding and racing of pigeons, some of these clubs still exist today. This shows members of the club with some of the trophies and their pigeons. Although most of the people here are unknown, there are some very well-known ones: Bert Soloman (3rd left front row), his brother 'Barney' Soloman (3rd right front row). The little boy is Llew Tamblyn with his father (1st left back row).

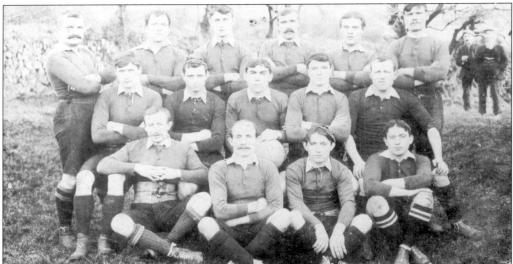

REDRUTH R.F.C. 1908. Formed in 1875, it is the second oldest club in the county. The pitch was the field beside the old Brewery Leats but later the club moved to the Recreation Ground where it has been ever since. Over the years the club has produced players who have represented their County and Country with great pride, men like Bert Soloman, Maffer Davey, Roy Jennings, Len Roberts and Dr Keith Scott. The following three photographs show the club during different periods of their history and players who have played their part in keeping the name of Redruth Rugby Club known all over the world. This team includes Bert Soloman (1st left middle row) and 'Maffer' Davey (Captain). Other well known players were Willie Job, Jackie Solomon, Frank Carbis, R. Jackett. This was also the year that Cornwall won the County Championship.

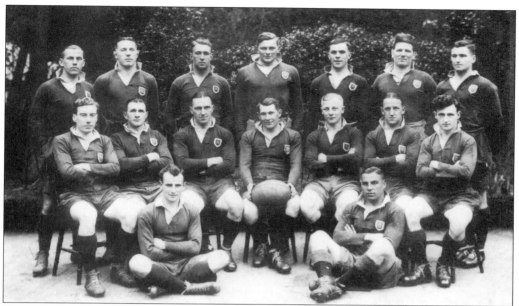

REDRUTH R.F.C. 1934-35. Back row, left to right: Ted Hitchens, Francis Gregory, Frank Roberts, Bill Phillips, Gordon Robbins, Leslie Semmens. Middle row: Len Roberts, Freddie Pappin, Roy Jennings, Percy Rogers, Harold Curnow, Ken Williams, 'Penno' Knowles. Front row: David Jones, Fred Bone.

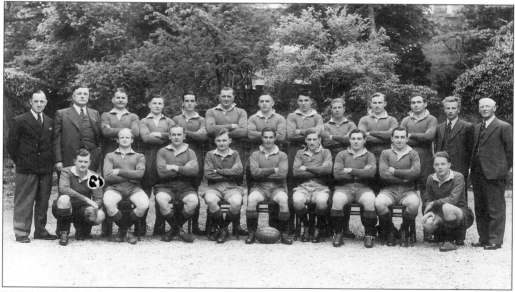

REDRUTH R.F.C. 1950-51. Back row, left to right: Ken Williams, John Richards, Eric Edmonds, Jack Gribble, John Knuckey, Bill Phillips, Tony Bidgood, Alan Mitchell, Willie Bone, Bob Lewis, Ivor Andrews, Raymond Hicks, Sam Scoble. Front row: Bert Solomon, Len Semmens, Harry Baker, Thurston Thomas, Frank Partridge (Captain), Keith Scott, Keith Eddy, Paddy Bradley, Bill Bishop.

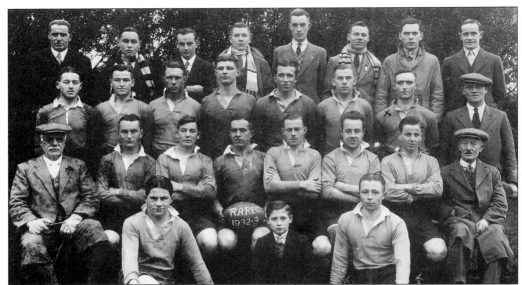

REDRUTH ALBANY 1932-33. Throughout the years many junior clubs existed in and around the Redruth district, some are still playing today whilst others have unfortunately ceased. It was these junior clubs that gave great support to the senior side, their efforts in maintaining the rugby tradition should always be remembered. Some of the sides that no longer exist are North Country, Four Lanes, Redruth Midgets, Redruth Highway, Lanner and Carharrack, whilst others like Redruth Albany and St Day still carry on their proud tradition. Back row, left to right: Mr Johnson, Bernard Woods, Jack Thomas, Clifton Braddock, Johnson Ellis, Sam Thomas, Tom Gerry, Jimmy Hodge. 1st row: Stuart Bath, Leslie Semmens, Frank Roberts, Jimmy O'Shea, Jimmy Newton, Teddy Hitchens, Reggie Ellis, Walter Words. 2nd row: Montague Jennings, Pat Matthews, Reggie Paul, Frank Thomas (Captain), Reggie Daddow, Herbert Hattam, Reggie Scoble, Mr Hattam. Front row: Jack Goldsworthy, ? Barnes (Mascot), Ralph Hattam.

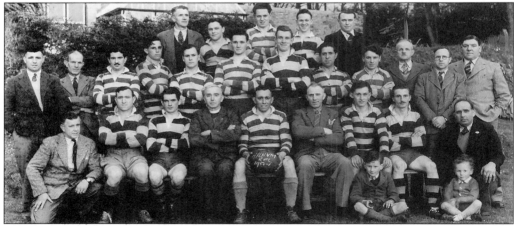

REDRUTH HIGHWAY 1950-51. Back row, left to right: Jack Pappin, Jack Bone, John Huxtable, Dennis Teague, Miles Bryant. Middle row: Leonard Allen, Henry Williams, Ernie Taylor, Alan Opie, Jack Golley, Bruce Maughflin, Peter Williams, 'Porky' Richards, Gerald Gribble, Mr Perry, Jack Angove, Jimmy Harris. Front row: George Hart, Ernie Eley, Norman Sedgeman, Reverend Hawthorn, Peter Rhys (Captain), Eddie Stewart, David Rowe, Les Tromans, Albert Jory.

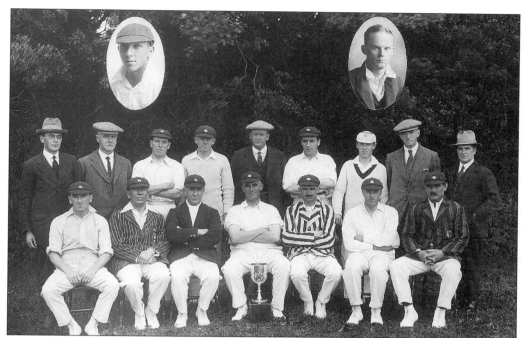

REDRUTH XI 1925, WINNERS OF THE COUNTY LEAGUE. Cricket was also very popular in the district. Although not achieving the success that the rugby club did, it nevertheless had some good years. The following photographs depict different eras of the club's history. Back row left to right: A. Paul, W. Painter, F. Thomas, L. Tamblyn, C. J. Cooke (President), W. Heeson, W. Pearce, T. Hughes, H. Griffin. Front row: W. Cory, H. Dransfield, L. Polglase, W. Nicholls (Captain), W. Matthews, E. Oates, C. Trevarthen. Insets: R. Jennings, E. Thomas.

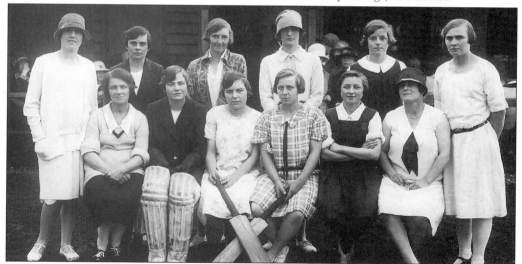

REDRUTH LADIES XI 1927. Forget male chauvinism, equal rights, etc, in 1927 a team of ladies played a match against a team of Redruth Vice-Presidents, most of whom were prominent businessmen of the town. The result was a fine win for the ladies by 61 runs to 50 runs. Back row, left to right: M. Griffin, E. Hosking, K. Chandler, M. Smith, M. Gill, F. Paul. Front row: G. Munday, A. Tamblyn, E. Hicks, M. Sara, L. Munday, D. Small.

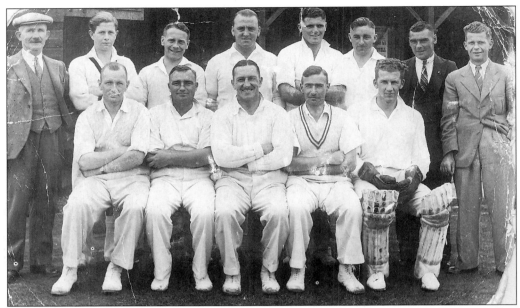

REDRUTH XI 1937-38. Back row, left to right: W. Prisk, B. Richards, K. Nicholls, C. Bradley, C. Howard, A. Gribble, W. Stephens, T. Harry. Front row: A. Choak, R. Palmer, R. Jennings, S. Willis, K. Hosking.

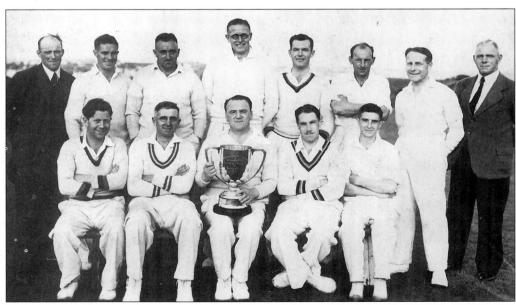

REDRUTH XI 1946, WINNERS OF THE COUNTY LEAGUE, WESTERN DIVISION. Back row, left to right: P. Ball (Scorer), F. Partridge, A. Gribble, F. Hobbs, W. Rich, C. Caseley, K. Nicholls, Colonel Osborne (President). Front row: B. Richards, J. E. Mill, C. Bradley (Captain), M. Tobin, E. Charleston.

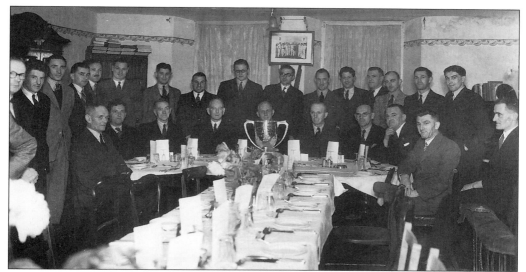

CELEBRATION DINNER. Taken at the Celebration Dinner held at the Red Lion Hotel, Fore Street when the officials of the County Cricket Club were present. Those seated are, left to right: Percy Ball, Bert Bennetts, F. G. Hughes, Arthur Lugg (County Secretary) Colonel H. Osborne (Club President), Frank Littlejohns (County Treasurer), Clifton Clark, C. M. Bradley (Club Captain), W. D. Cory.

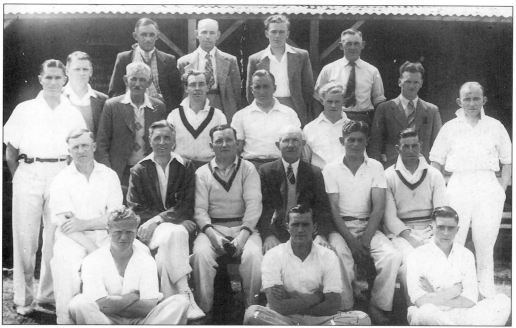

REDRUTH DISTRICT XI 1944. At the end of the war when cricket clubs were starting up once again, members of various clubs amalgamated to play a match on the Redruth ground. Back row, left to right : F. Spurr, A. Polkinhorne, B. Tremberth, W. Hoone. 1st row: F. Partridge, T. Wignall, C. Johns, A. Penna, A. Gribble, J. Pascoe, F. Bawden, A. Williams. 2nd row: J. Cooke, H. Needham, B. Bennetts, W. Prisk (President), F. Bray, A. James. Front row: W. Job, W. Pappin, E. Charleston.

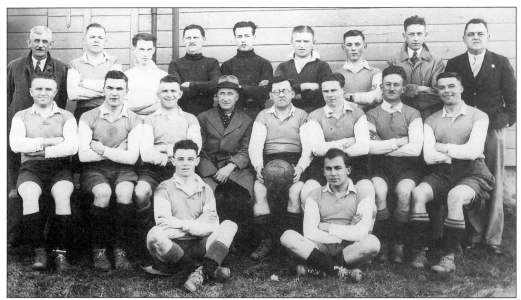

REDRUTH POST OFFICE FOOTBALL XI 1935. Rugby was not the only type of football played in the town, although the 'round ball' game was not as popular, there were nevertheless several soccer teams around. Looking at this picture one could imagine the captain, Bert Bennetts, in some difficulty once he took his glasses off! Back row, left to right: C. Johns, G. Matthews, H. Smith, E. Dunn, A. Osborne, R. Goldsworthy, C. Jeffrey, V. Brown, W. Argall. Middle row: K. Goldsworthy, A. Hocking, W. Vinnicombe, H. Osborne, B. Bennett (Captain), B. Richards, A. Uren, L. Exelby. Front row: A. Rowlands, B. Carter.

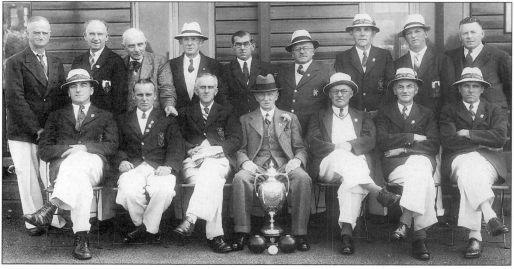

REDRUTH BOWLING CLUB 1940. Another of the very popular pastimes that one could take part in. The Bowling Club had its headquarters and green at Victoria Park. This team shows the result of a successful year by displaying the Nicholls Cup. Back row, left to right: F. Salter, W. Chudleigh, A. H. Opie, A. Benny, W. Thomas, F. Venton, J. Davey, E. Reed, W. Webster. Front row: J. Thomas, S. Exelby (Secretary), H. Downing (Captain), W. Treloar (President), E. Trewren (Vice Captain), W. Tiddy, J. Eddy.

Three
Religion
Chapels and Churches

The history of Religion in Redruth has, fortunately, been well documented from the earliest of the known churches, the parish church at St Euny (1259) to the newer church at St Andrews (1883). Although the chapels are not so old, for some reason they seem to have a special meaning to the people of the district. Whether it was the method of preaching or the charisma of the preacher, there were certainly more chapels than churches.

The following selection of photographs will, I hope, stir happy memories of the many chapels now closed, the Tea Treats with the cup of tea and saffron bun and maybe even a trip to the seaside at Carbis Bay – many happy cherished memories.

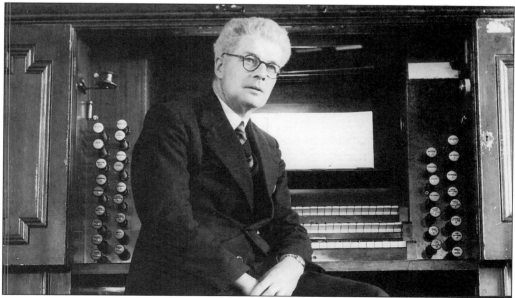

DONALD BROAD. A very well-known and accomplished musician and organist seen here seated at the organ of the Flowerpot chapel.

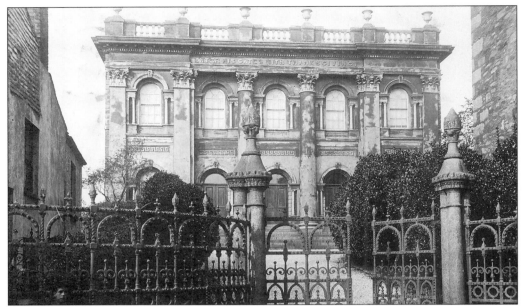

U.M.F.C. "FLOWERPOT" CHAPEL. Although not the oldest chapel in the town, it was perhaps the most well known, built in 1865, it became known as "Flowerpot" because of the large ornamental pots on the balustrade. It was also known as the "Cathedral of Methodism". During the 1939-45 war it became home to the Marylebone Grammar School from London and then one night in 1973 a fire completely gutted the building. Along with the Trounson Memorial Hall, it was pulled down and is now the site of a car park.

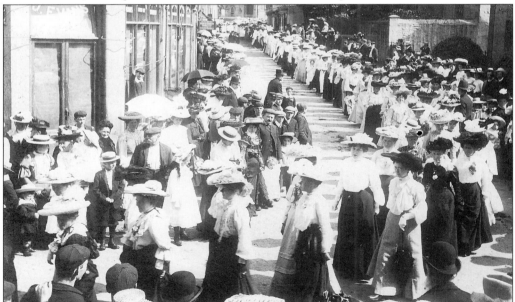

U.M.F.C. TEA TREAT, 1905. Part of the chapels' festivities included the annual Tea Treat – here the Ladies Section are seen parading through Penryn Street in all their finery. Sometimes they would go to Carbis Bay and the beach, other times they would go to the fields of Penventon House where tea and saffron buns would be served.

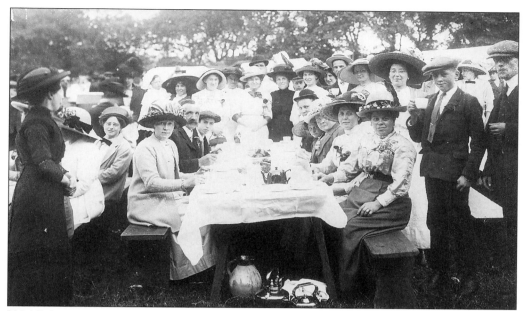

U.M.F.C. TEA TREAT, 1913. Having completed their parade around the streets, members of the "Flowerpot" Chapel are seen here enjoying cups of tea and saffron buns in the grounds of Penventon House.

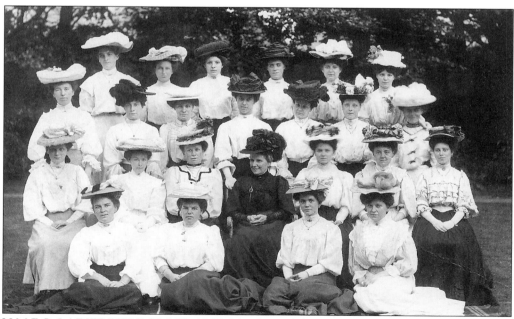

U.M.F.C. LADIES BIBLE CLASS, 1907. Members of the U.M.F.C. Bible Class dressed in all their finery. The lady in the black dress is Mrs Tom Trounson.

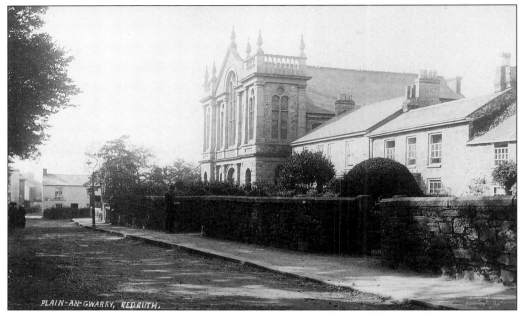

PRIMITIVE METHODIST: PLAIN-AN-GWARRY. This beautifully fronted chapel was built in 1884. Now like many others, the doors are closed, the choir stalls are empty and the congregation has gone. It stands awaiting its fate.

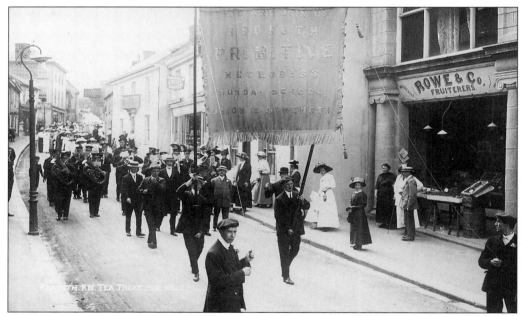

PRIMITIVE METHODIST TEA TREAT. Another of the marvellous tea treats, taken at West End, it is possible they are returning to the chapel after the days outing. In those days (1913) the tea treat would have been held in the grounds of Tolvean House, the home of the Lanyon family. Whatever happened to the lovely banners that used to be at the head of all the parades?

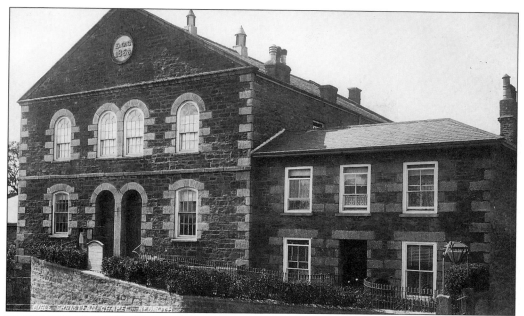

TRERUFFE CHAPEL. Home of the Bible Christian section of the United Methodist Chapel, it was situated in Treruffe Hill. Opened in 1863, it is now unfortunately closed.

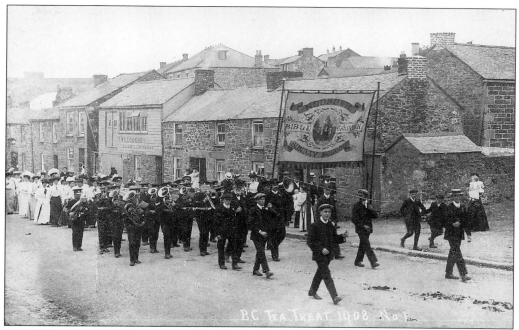

TRERUFFE CHAPEL TEA TREAT. Another of the beautifully ornate banners leading out the Redruth Band and members of the chapel whilst parading up Falmouth Road.

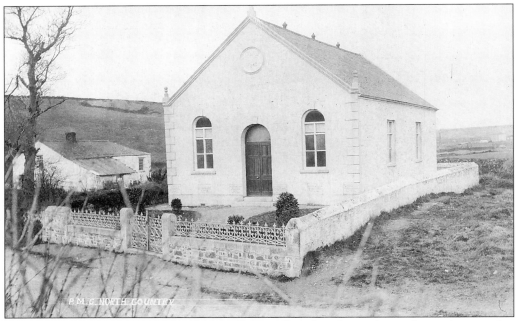

LOWER NORTH COUNTRY. One of the smaller chapels in the outlying district, this particular building is situated on the cross roads of Lower North Country and Portreath Road. Although closed for services it is now being used as a Chapel of Rest.

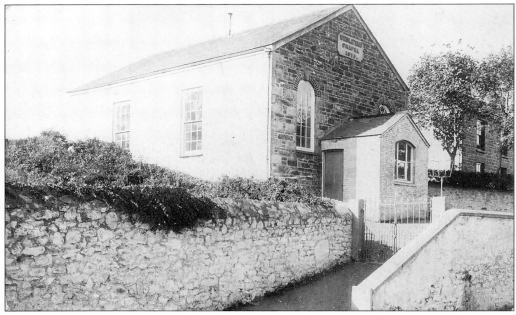

CARN BREA CHAPEL. This little chapel founded in 1870 is one of the few smaller Wesleyan buildings still enjoying regular services.

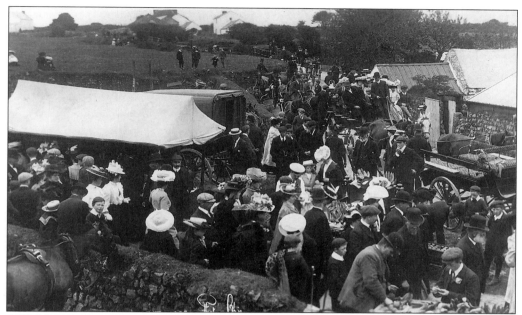

GWENNAP PIT. This natural amphitheatre about one and a half miles east of Redruth is known throughout the world. It has been known as the "Mecca of Methodism" and is a source of great faith to those who have attended the annual Whit-Monday service. The acoustics of the "Pit" are remarkable, the singing reverberates all around. In 1931, breaking an age old tradition that only Wesleyan Methodists could preach to the assembly, the Reverend E. Bennett, a United Methodist, preached to a crowd of some 6,000 people. The two pictures show firstly the crowd arriving outside the "Pit" in all methods of horse drawn transport, secondly the crowd assembled listening to the preacher giving his sermon.

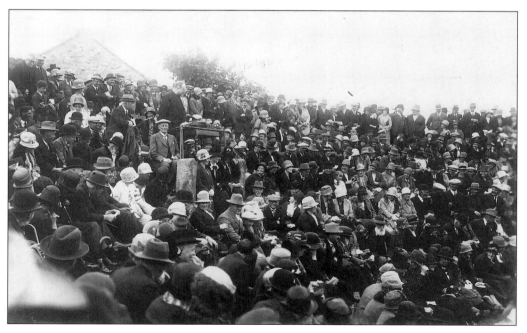

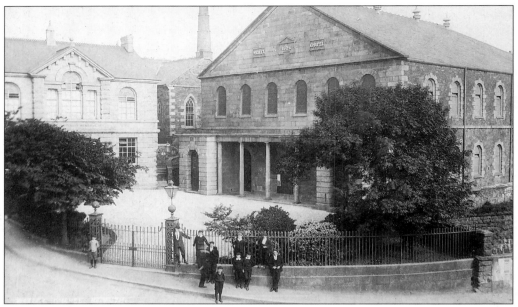

WESLEY CHAPEL. This was, and is, the senior of the Wesleyan chapels in the town, the present building built in 1826 is the third on this site. Known as the "Mother of all the Wesleys", the chapel could seat as many as 1,400 people. The building to the left is the Wesley Centenary building, used as the Sunday School for some time. The dominating stack in the background is that of the old Pednandrea Mine.

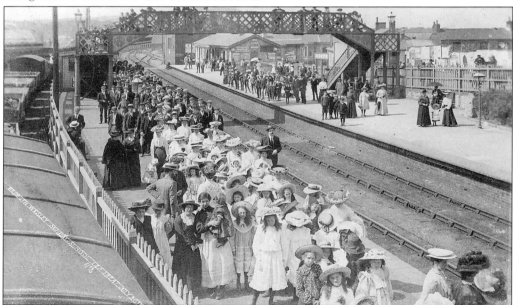

WESLEY CHAPEL TEA TREAT. Once again the annual tea treat is well supported, here members are gathered on the platform of the railway station waiting for the Tea Treat Special to arrive to take them to Carbis Bay. What a day out it must have been, a ride in a lovely old G.W.R. steam engine, beautiful sunshine, the sea and of course the saffron bun - what memories.

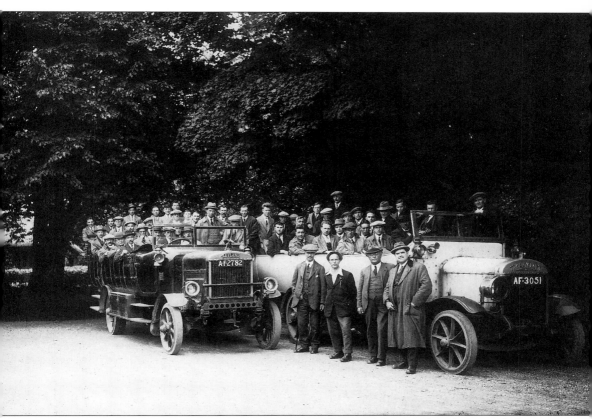

WESLEY CHAPEL YOUNG MENS BIBLE CLASS (Y.M.B.C.). Another feature of the Wesley Chapel was their very large and successful Y.M.B.C., run with great vigour by Mr Harry Rich. This group of people made journeys to various parts of Devon and Cornwall. Here we see two old charabancs fully loaded and ready for a trip to Restormel and Launceston. Mr Harry Rich is standing second from the right.

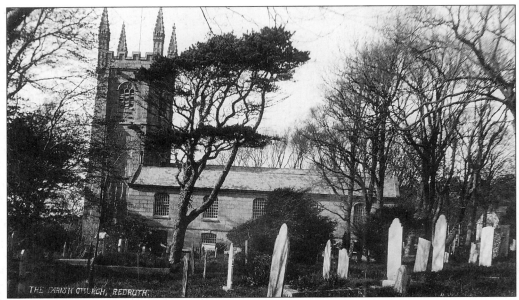

ST. EUNY CHURCH. This historic church (1259) is the oldest building in the town, still being used for its original purpose. As it stands now it is the third church built here, foundations of a Norman Church (c.1100) were found beneath the present nave. The tower stands at its highest point some 86 feet from the ground and looks out over the lovely quiet village of Carn Brea. Church services are held regularly and the sound of the bells can be heard for many a mile.

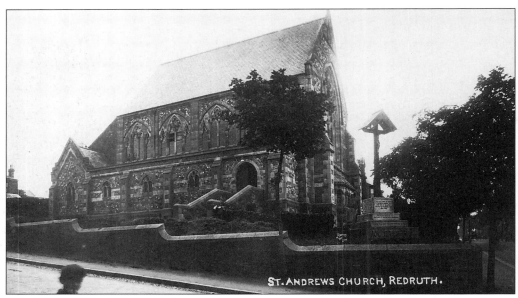

ST ANDREWS CHURCH. For many years it was realized that the Parish Church was somewhat remote from the town, other places like St Rumons Chapel and the Chapel of Ease were used but not found to be satisfactory. In 1880 it was first mooted that another church was necessary, thus the idea of St Andrews came to fruition. 1883 saw the laying of the foundation stone and the church was eventually consecrated in 1884. This picture shows the church as it was before the alterations of 1937-38.

64

Four

Events
Some Happy, Some Sad

It is difficult to imagine what it was like in earlier days, no TV or wireless, and none of today's other distractions. People made their own amusements. The following selection of photographs shows events which drew crowds of various sizes – some happy times, others with more distressful results. From the very large agricultural show to the local fete, the Royal visit to the Whitsun Fair, from the house fire to the mine subsidence – all in their own way were something special.

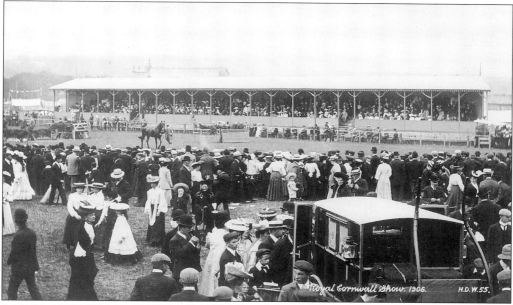

ROYAL CORNWALL SHOW 1906. The Royal Cornwall Show in its early days never had a permanent home, unlike today with the large ground at Wadebridge. The show travelled around the county, from Saltash and Launceston in the east to Penzance and St Ives in the west, changing its venue from year to year. After its formation in 1793 the Royal Cornwall Show came to Redruth on four occasions - 1881,1892 1906 and 1952. The following three views show scenes from the 1906 event held on the Redruth Recreation Ground, a site owned by the Redruth Exhibition Committee. A general view looking across the horse jumping arena to a grandstand packed with spectators, altogether some 20,000 people attended that year. In the foreground people dressed in their Sunday best inspect the local horse-drawn ambulance.

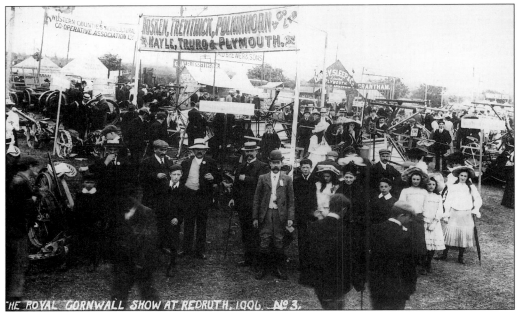

THE ROYAL CORNWALL SHOW AT REDRUTH, 1906. Nº 3.

THE FARM MACHINERY SECTION. One of the most important sections of the show was the farm machinery. Here farmers could see the latest equipment on offer, the local suppliers of traction engines, ploughs, binders and many others, all advertising their own particular speciality.

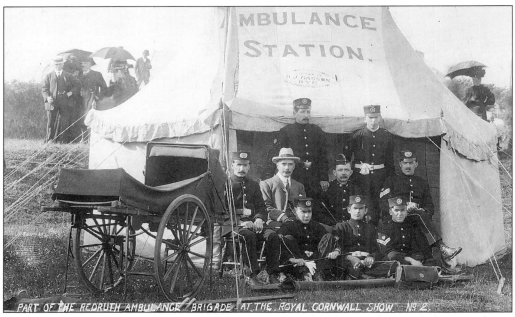

PART OF THE REDRUTH AMBULANCE BRIGADE AT THE ROYAL CORNWALL SHOW Nº 2.

ST JOHNS AMBULANCE. As with all major events today the St Johns Ambulance is always on hand and ready to give assistance when required. Here members of the brigade pose outside their station with the mobile handcart-cum-stretcher waiting for the first casualty. The four seated are, left to right: Serg Hattam, Dr Laurie (Div Surg), Supt Parsons, Sgt James.

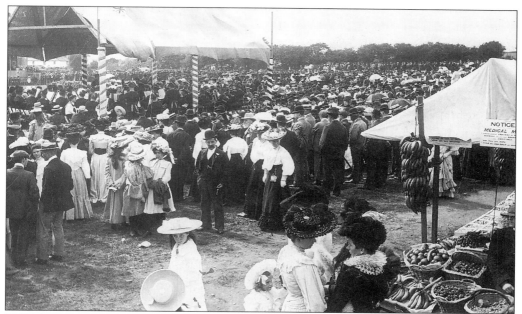

REDRUTH EXHIBITION. This picture and the following three are of Redruth Exhibition. It was very similar to the Royal Cornwall Show, was spread over two days and attracted very large crowds. A general view with large crowds listening to the band of H.M. Grenadier Guards.

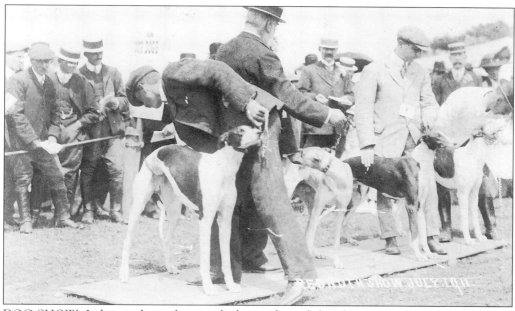

DOG SHOW. Judging taking place, with the greyhounds lined up and waiting to be given an inspection by one of the judges.

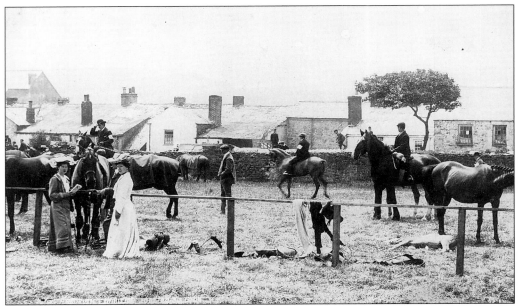

HORSE SHOW. Riders and their mounts warming up behind the grandstand, or is it the mare and foal section?

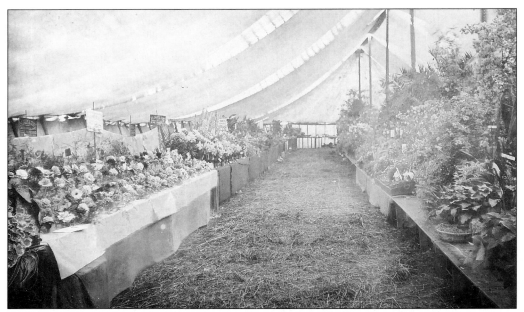

THE FLOWER TENT. This large tent has been laid out for the flower section of the show. Here parts of that exhibition shows how popular these displays were. The notices on the left indicate – B.R. Davies, Begonia Specialist, Yeovil.

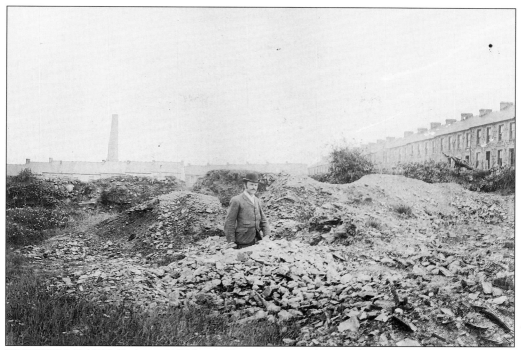

VICTORIA PARK. Early in 1897 Lord Clinton gave to the people of Redruth a parcel of land approximately six acres in size to layout as a park. Looking at this picture it is difficult to believe that for £500 it was transformed into a beautiful park. The gentleman standing in the middle is Mr Joseph Rich. In the background is the stack of the Pednandrea Mine.

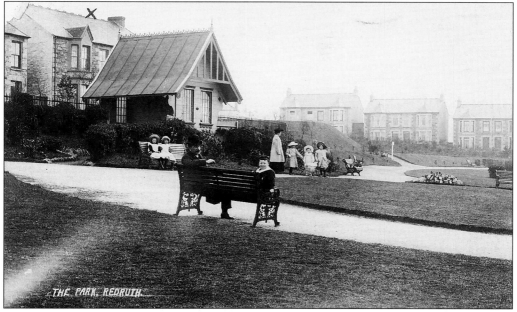

VICTORIA PARK. People enjoying the peace and tranquillity of the park. Looking from the centre of the layout towards what is now the Bowling Green.

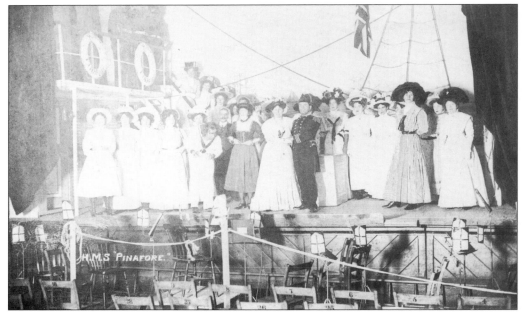

THE OPERATIC SOCIETY. On stage at the Druids Hall are the cast of the Redruth Operatic Society after their performance of *H.M.S. Pinafore*.

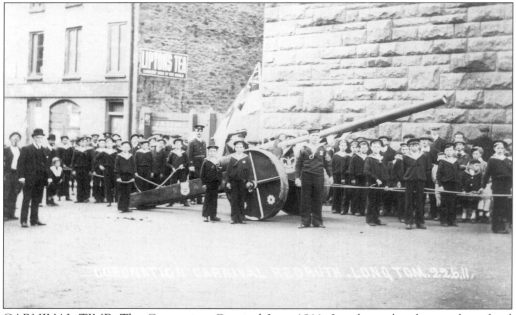

CARNIVAL TIME. The Coronation Carnival June 1911. Local naval cadets ready to haul "Long Tom" in the procession from here, under the viaduct in Falmouth Road, down to the Recreation Ground. With other sections of the Carnival the cadets took part in various sports and games and afterwards Coronation mugs were handed out to everyone.

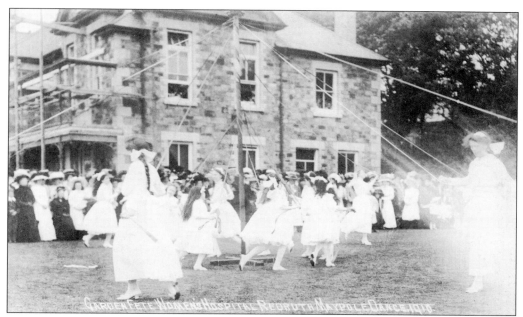

REDRUTH HOSPITAL FETE. Signs of happier moments at the Annual Garden Fete of the Womens Hospital, one of the traditional Maypole dances held on the lawn. The Womens Hospital opened in 1890 when it was intended that preference should be given to women who worked in the mines and tin streams. For many years the hospital went from strength to strength and in doing so it achieved a first class record. Now that we know it will soon close, we can remember the doctors, nurses and ancillary workers for the fine service they provided.

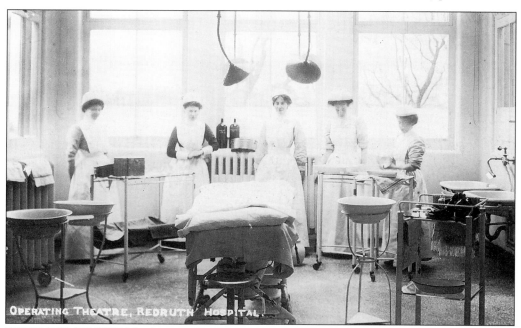

REDRUTH HOSPITAL. A view that not many patients saw, the operating theatre and staff. Few of today's modern aids were available, nevertheless, a tremendous job of work was done.

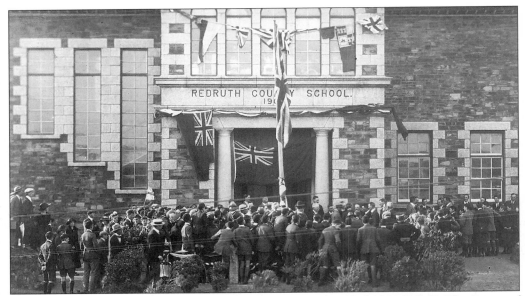

ROYAL VISIT H.R.H. THE PRINCE OF WALES. On May 23rd 1921 H.R.H. The Prince of Wales made history in being the first member of royalty to visit the town. On a tour of the western part of the county, he called at various towns. At Redruth he was welcomed by crowds estimated to be over 20,000. The Prince of Wales' first call was at the Redruth County School. Here he was introduced to principal townspeople and council officials, school children from the County School, Trewirgie, East End and Treleigh were also present, together with Crimean war veteran James Hocking and his wife.

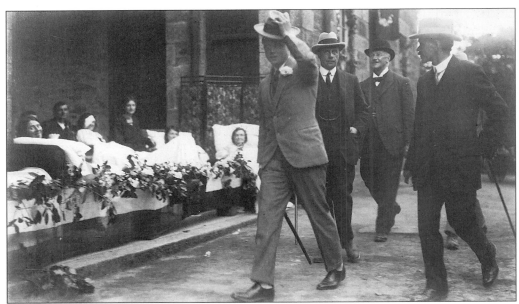

MINERS AND WOMENS HOSPITAL. The Prince is seen here with some of the patients at the hospital as well. As meeting representatives of the Hospital Committee he opened a new extension which was to be accommodation for the nursing staff.

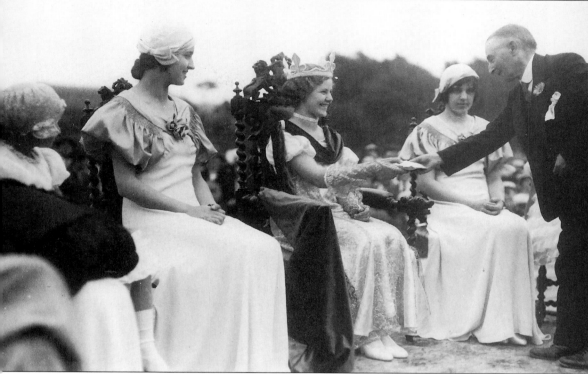

CROWNING THE CARNIVAL QUEEN. Another happy occasion held at the Recreation Ground, after a long carnival had paraded around the town judging for the queen took place. This particular crowning was in 1933 when Muriel Yelland was successful. Here she is receiving her prize from Mr Howarth. A Miss P. Mugford and Emily Mitchell were the two attendants with Barbara Jennings and Mary Penna as train bearers.

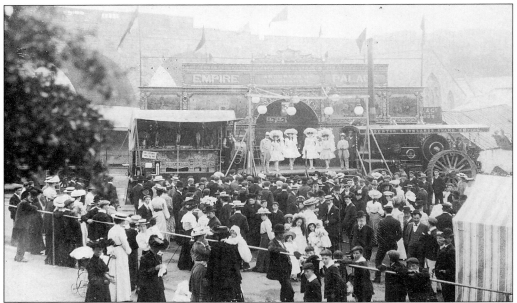

ANDERTON AND ROWLAND EMPIRE PALACE. Popular visitors to Redruth for many years have been the Fairs – Anderton and Rowland, Hancocks, M. & B. Hill are the most well-known. Each had their own special venue, West End Fair field, Fair Meadow in Station Hill and the Recreation Ground, plus some other smaller places, all contriving to give maximum entertainment. During the 1911 Coronation all three major fairs were held in Redruth at the same time and with rides at 1d a go it must have been a fun-filled few days. The following pictures show some of the different rides and attractions that were available. Taken in the Fair Meadow, Station Hill, this shows Anderton and Rowlands famous Dancing Girls lined up on stage ready for the next performance. Entrance fee was 3d. On the right can be seen one of the very large traction engines used to generate the power to operate the lighting and musical organ on the left.

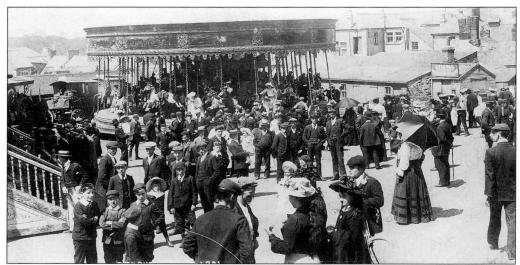

THE GALLOPERS. Another view at the Fair Meadow and the very popular Gallopers ride.

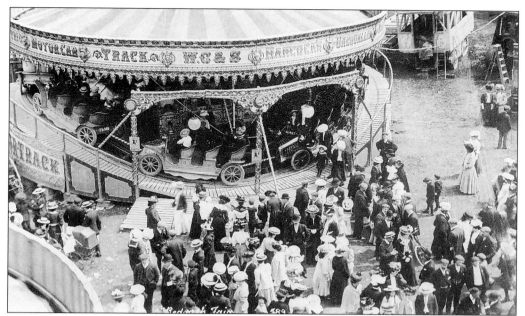

MOTOR CAR TRACK. The lovely motor car ride of Sophie Hancock at the West End Fair Ground. All aboard for only 1d a ride.

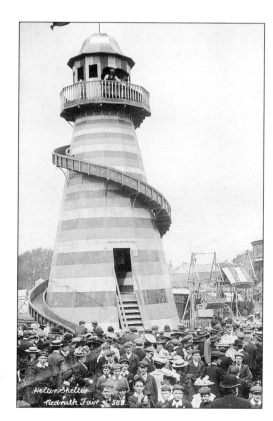

HELTER SKELTER. Nobody seems to want a ride on this beautiful Helter Skelter even at only 1d a go.

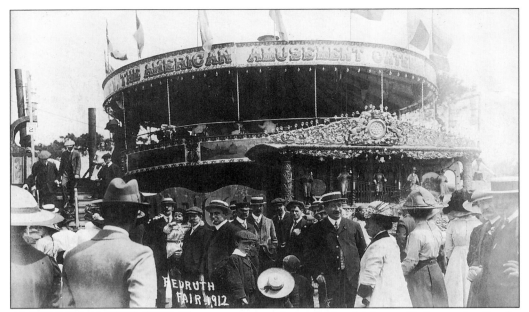

AMERICAN AMUSEMENT. This was a new and novel ride which provided great fun for the crowd as well as those riding. Apart from going around and around, it dipped up and down like a boat. If you were unprepared for these movements you were likely to be thrown out onto the floor.

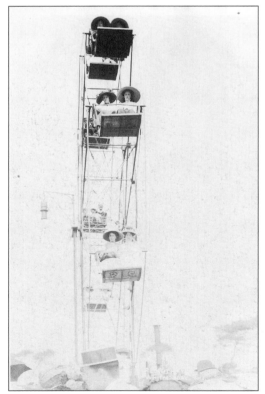

BIG WHEEL. Marshall and Bernard Hills Fair was held at the Recreation Ground. Looking at this picture of the Big Wheel makes one feel nervous. It was 60ft high and does not look very robust and with a strong wind blowing it would shake the strongest of constitutions.

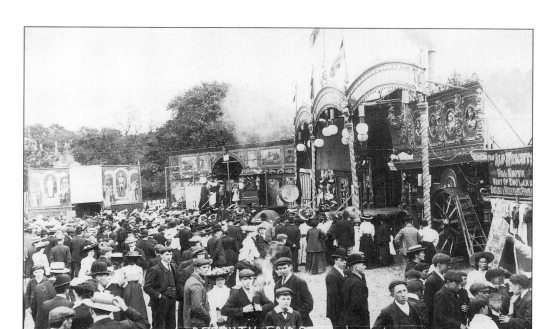

HANCOCKS LIVING PICTURES. Hancocks Variety and Bioscope Show at the West End, possibly the forerunner of the modern cinema, crowds could see for the first time animated scenes. Again one of the large traction engines, Burrell "Lord Roberts" providing power for the electricity.

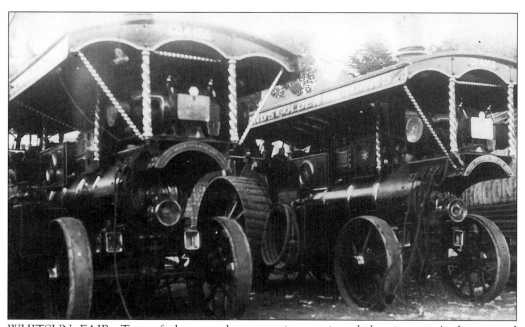

WHITSUN FAIR. Two of the very large traction engines belonging to Anderton and Rowlands at the Whitsun Fair. The engines were used to create the power to operate some of the fairground attractions.

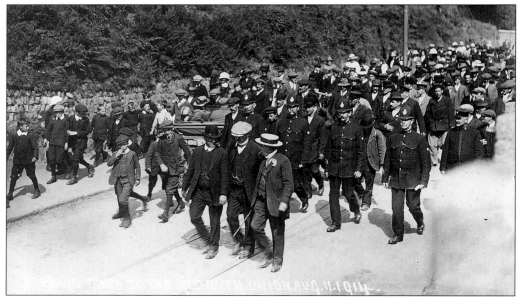

GERMAN PRISONERS, AUGUST 1914. One of the more unusual sights to have been seen was that of some German prisoners of war. These were men that had been passengers on a German ship, the *Kronprinzessen Cecille*. Having been escorted into Falmouth Harbour the men were taken off and brought to Redruth where they were marched under police escort to the workhouse. Three days later they were marched to the railway station, under military escort with fixed bayonets, and put on a train to Devonport. From there they were sent on to Salisbury Plain where they were interned for the duration of the war. This picture shows them marching down West End, outside the County School, on their way to Barncoose.

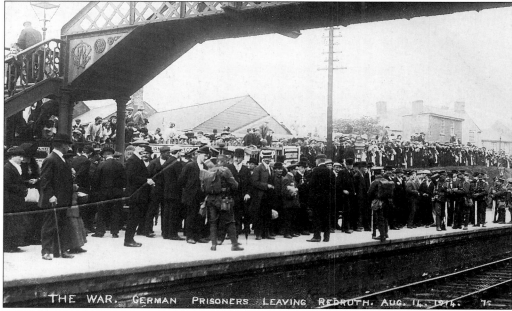

REDRUTH STATION. Assembled on the "Up" platform, prisoners under escort wait for their train.

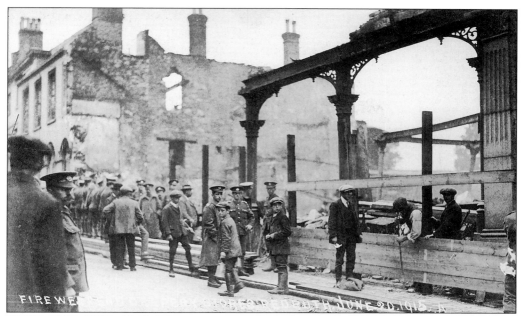

WEST END FIRE, 1915. This was a very large fire, with damage estimated at between £40/50,000 done to the West End Drapery Stores and the adjacent property. The local fire brigade, ably supported by units from Truro and Camborne, restricted the damage but it was, nevertheless, extensive. Seen from the bottom of West End, this shows the aftermath as a group of DCLIs assist in the clearing up.

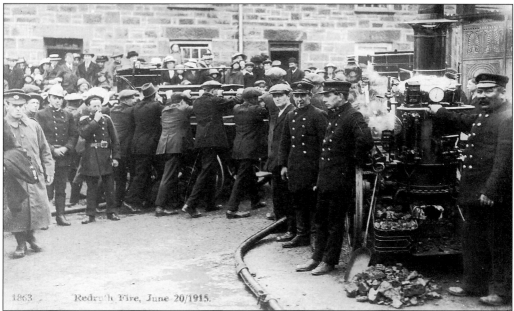

ALL HANDS TO THE PUMPS. Part of the Redruth Brigade with their Merryweather Steam Engine set up at the rear of Fore Street by Goodmans Workshop (side of the Regal Cinema) with some volunteers pumping water. The fireman on the right is the stoker of the brigade, it was his job to see that there was sufficient pressure to operate the pumps.

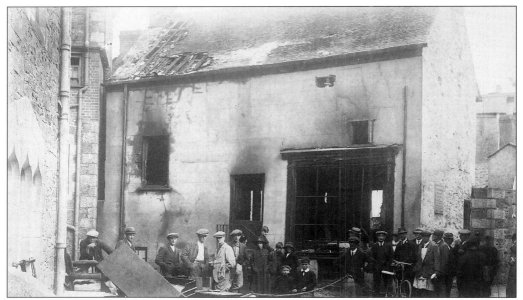

MURDOCH HOUSE. Scene of the disaster that occurred at Murdoch House in 1920. Taken just after the fire, all that remains are three walls and most of the roof. After this incident Mr Pearce Jenkin purchased the property and after restoration, various groups, including the Redruth Old Cornwall Society, used the building for meetings.

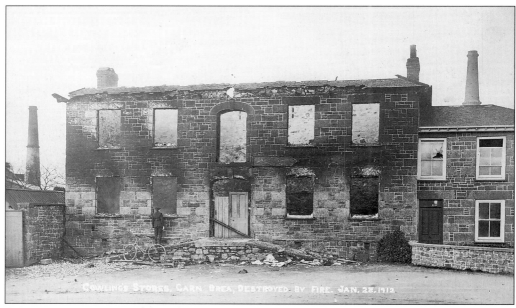

COWLINGS STORE. Although not in the central part of Redruth, Cowlings Store or Mill at Carn Brea was another building that suffered fire damage. In recent years the building has been completely renovated and is now the headquarters of Groundwork Kerrier, a group which is involved with restoration of our mining heritage and other projects. They have an interesting Discovery Centre at this site which is well worth a visit.

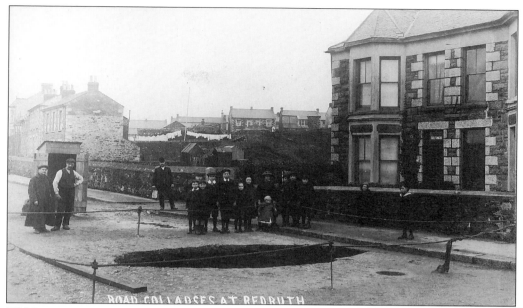

TREFUSIS ROAD. Another type of disaster that has been seen a few times over the years is that of mine subsidence. This view shows subsidence at the crossroads of Trefusis road and Park road where a hole has been fenced off and guarded.

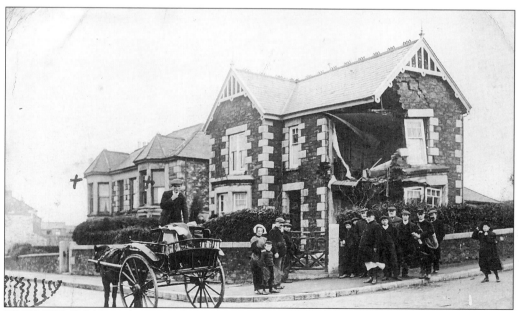

TREFUSIS ROAD. The second view shows that this large house has also suffered severe damage, the whole of the corner disappearing down the shaft. Fortunately no one was sleeping in the "spare room" at the time. Later the whole of the building was pulled down.

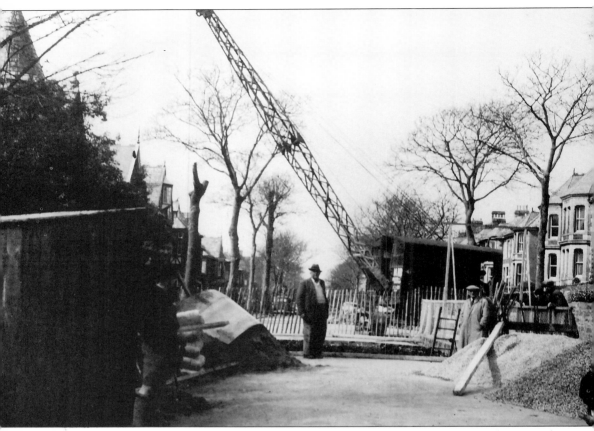

CLINTON ROAD. This collapse in 1955 caused severe disruption for six months, near the junction of Sparnon Hill and Park Road. A very deep hole appeared which was thought to be connected with the Old Wheal Sparnon Mine. Several other examples of subsidence occurred near here in 1911 and 1918.

Five

Mines in and around Redruth

Redruth was known for some time as the "Capital of the richest mining area in Cornwall", with mines stretching from Wheal Peevor in the north, Treskerby in the east, Bassets in the south and Illogan in the west, all producing tin and copper. Just as important was the employment they provided for thousands of people.

The following photographs show some of the mines in that area.

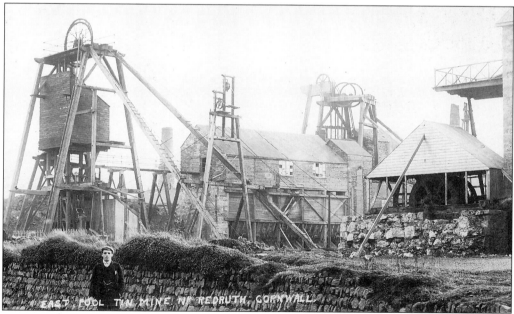

EAST POOL. A view from the old A30 road between Redruth and Camborne. This was quite an old mine as records show, going back to the seventeenth century – it was also very successful. This view shows Mitchells shaft headgear on the left, the rock breaking plant and beam winding engine on the right. The winding engine house has now been preserved by the National Trust.

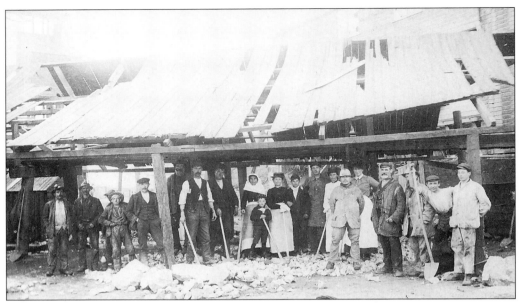

EAST POOL. A group of miners and ground workers from East Pool. Note the "Bal Maidens" in the centre.

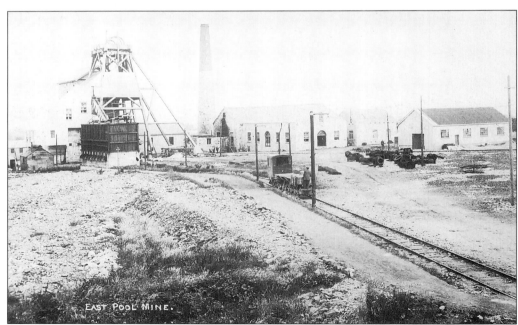

EAST POOL AND AGAR LIMITED. Looking down from where the Safeway Supermarket is now situated, this shows a general view of Taylors shaft and headgear around the mid 1920s. See the mineral tram returning from off-loading ore at the large milling and tin dressing plant at Tolvaddon.

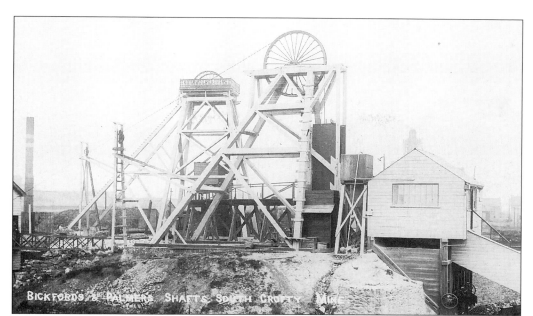

BICKFORD AND PALMERS SHAFTS - SOUTH CROFTY. This interesting view of these two old shafts was taken from Station Road in Pool looking west. Bickfords shaft is on the right, Palmers on the left. The old office buildings and yards would have been to the right of the small hut. Due to an influx of funds in 1906, South Crofty Company started modernising and Robinsons shaft, with the associated headgear, etc., was built to replace the old Palmers shaft.

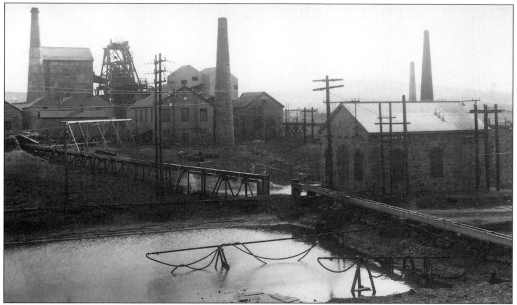

SOUTH CROFTY. A general view of Cooks Shaft at South Crofty, now the only working mine left in the county. Known as South Crofty Limited, it came into being in 1906. The photograph, taken in the early 1920s, shows Cooks shaft and headgear on the left, the mill house in the centre and calciners stacks on the right behind the power house. In the foreground is one of the low level water reservoirs.

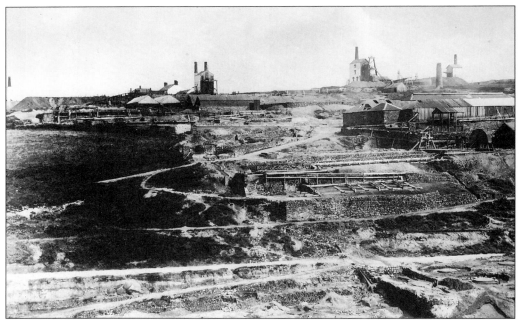

WHEAL UNY. A wonderful view of the Wheal Uny complex, situated to the south of Redruth overlooking the old Parish Church. This was taken just about the time when the mine was being abandoned, it shows Hinds pump and winding engine house on the right and the old stamps engine house in the centre. The centre right of picture shows some very extensive dressing works and the road from St Euny Parish Church to Carnkie is in the foreground.

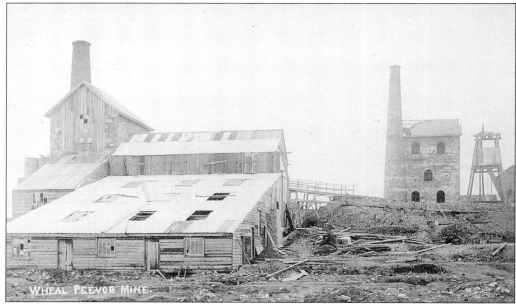

WHEAL PEEVOR. These old engine houses can still be seen today from the new A30 dual carriageway near the Avers interchange, north of Redruth. The scene is of dereliction, the old pumping house with half the roof missing, headgear standing idle and the stamps and dressing floor buildings all having seen better days.

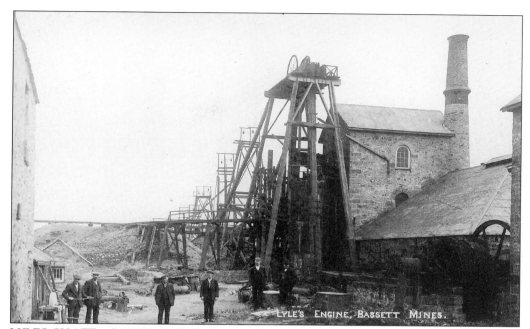

LYLES SHAFT - BASSET MINE. Situated between the village of Carnkie and Carn Brea, Lyles shaft formed the North Basset section of the mine. It had a large 80 inch pumping engine, seen here in the centre of the picture. The large high pulley frames were used to support the winding ropes going back to the engine some 200 yards away. In the front right is an old beam winding engine which was used to lift heavy machinery in the shaft.

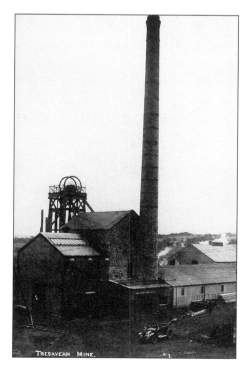

TRESAVEAN MINE - LANNER. As one travels through the village of Lanner towards Falmouth on the hill to the right can still be seen signs of this mine. Taken in 1912 this photograph shows the tallest mine stack in the county (150ft), with the winding house of Harveys shaft close by. Tresavean in its early days was an extremely efficient and profitable copper producer, it was hoped that by installing a new electric generating plant, tin might be found to be just as productive.

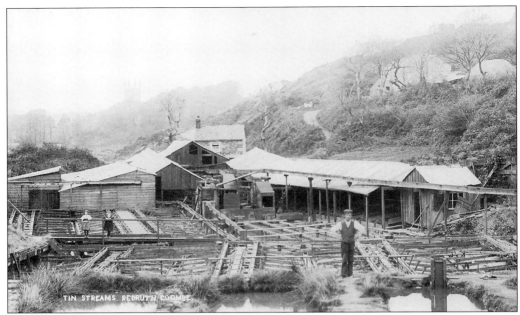

TIN STREAMING - REDRUTH COOMBE. The process of extracting tin at the mines allowed for some tin to be lost and tin streaming was a method used to recover as much of this "lost" mineral as possible. The site seen here was in the valley between Wheal Uny and Carn Brea. The Parish Church can be seen in the background. These works would not only recover tin deposit from the Basset group of mines but quite possibly the Wheal Uny group as well.

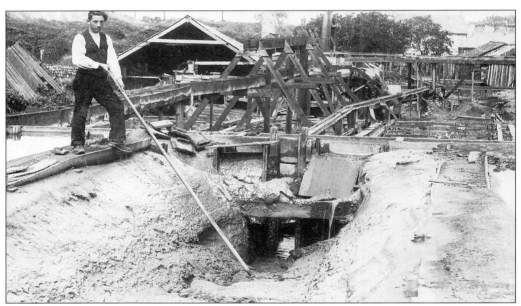

TIN STREAMING. Another part of the process was the cleaning out of the slime pits. This man is re-treating accumulated tin bearing material, easing the waste through the open gateway into the next section of the works. This tin streaming plant was in the Pool/Tolvaddon area.

Six

Transport From the Horse to Motor Car

To many people personal transport means a motor car, a train or even a bus but in earlier days it meant a pony and trap, a Landau or a Jersey wagon, a steam wagon, traction engine or even a tram. Wherever one intended to travel, there was always some type of transport for the occasion. I have tried to include in this section as wide a range of transport photographs as possible. These will bring back memories to some and to others they will appear a little strange. They form a part of the history of transport within the area.

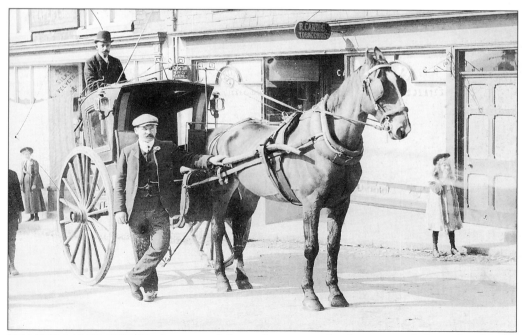

HANSOM CAB 1910/12. An unusual form of transport for this area, it belonged to Hicks, Butchers and Sweetmakers of Higher Fore Street. This Hansom cab is standing outside the entrance to the Tunnel Stores.

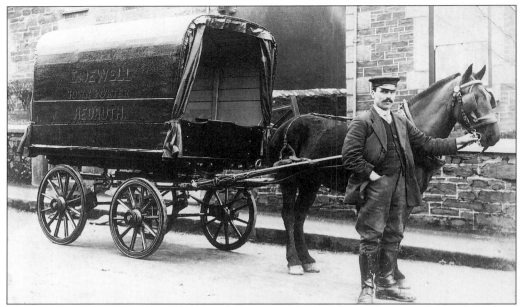

TOWN PORTER 1912. Mr Jewell, Town Porter. One of his functions was to collect and deliver large trunks, suitcases and other goods mainly from the railway station and deliver them to wherever passengers required them. He would also be available for other duties in the town such as making deliveries for businesses whose customers lived in outlying districts.

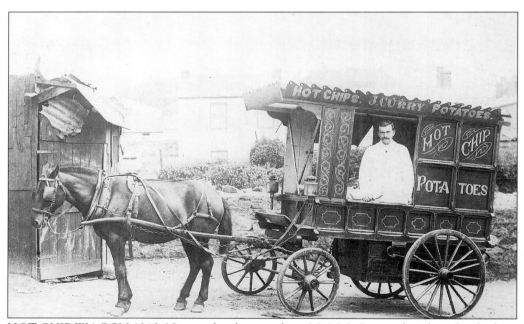

HOT CHIP WAGON 1910. Not much is known about Mr M. J. Curry other than that he kept his horse and wagon in the Plain-an-Gwarry area of Redruth. This form of transport was obviously the forerunner of the motorised fish and chip vans even though travelling in it must have been quite dangerous.

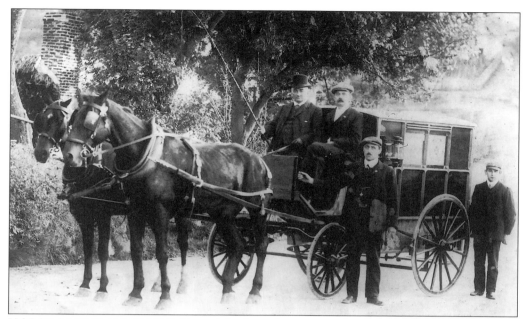

HORSE AMBULANCE 1916. One of the first of its type in the district, this old horse drawn ambulance was christened the "Humanity" when dedicated in 1906. It was kept with the horses in stables at Tabbs Hotel yard. Members of the Brigade in the picture are, left to right: Mr John Hugo (driver and owner of the stables), Supt. Parsons, F. James and W. Lanyon.

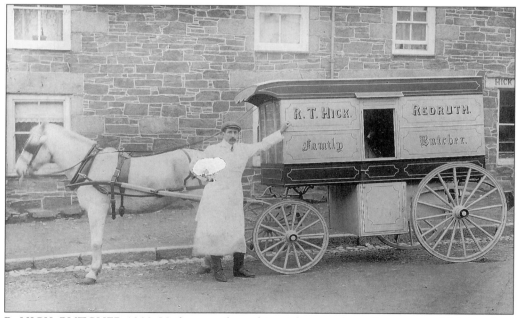

R. HICK, BUTCHER 1908. Unfortunately nothing is known about the owners of this butchers wagon but it is a typical example of the type used during this period.

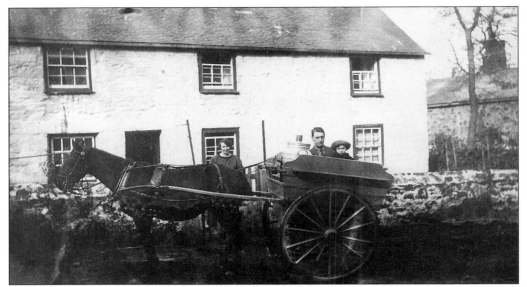

G. REED, MILKMAN 1926. Taken outside Town Farm in Falmouth Road, Mr George Reed with son, Brian, are ready to start off on their rounds whilst Mrs Reed looks on. The trap has been loaded with a large milk churn. No doubt the hand can and measures are on board ready for the first customers.

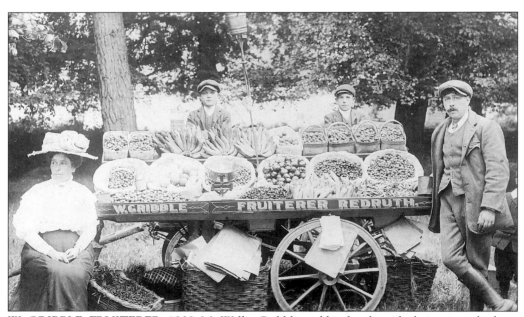

W. GRIBBLE, FRUITERER, 1908. Mr Willie Gribble and his family with their wagon laid out with all types of fruit. As well as having a regular stall on market days outside Lloyds Bank, he would be seen at many of the local shows and feasts. Note the old naptha lamp for use in the darker evenings.

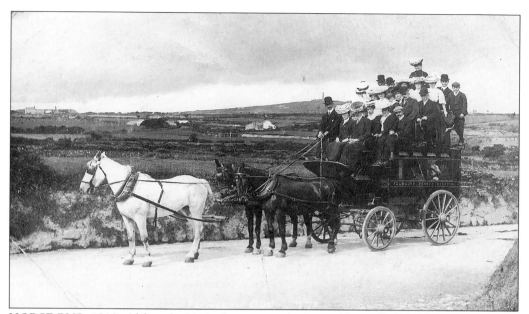

HORSE BUS, 1910. Although this is the wagon which would usually have been used on the Redruth-Falmouth route, it looks as though, on this occasion, it is being used for a works outing. It is pictured at South Downs with a full load, twenty two people riding outside and all seats taken inside. Pity the poor horses if they were having to go down Lanner Hill! The driver of this wagon is Bert Tallack.

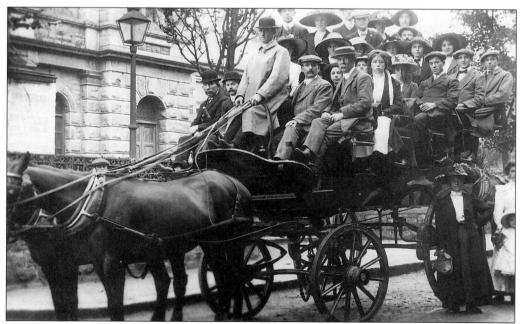

JERSEY WAGON, 1910. Sunday Schools had their tea-treats, chapel choirs and outings. This is the Plain-an-Gwarry Primitive Methodist Chapel Choir on their annual outing using a Jersey wagon of the Redruth Excursion Company.

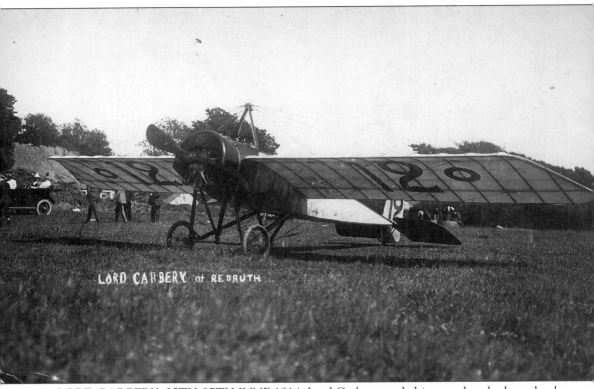

LORD CARBERY of REDRUTH

LORD CARBERY, 25TH-27TH JUNE 1914. Lord Carbery made history when he brought the first aeroplane to Redruth. The body of the plane, a Morane-Saulnier 80 HP monoplane, was taken by lorry to Sinns Barton Farm where the wings were attached. During the three days, Lord Carbery gave flying demonstrations which included Looping the Loop and Upside down flying, plus trips for passengers around the countryside.

Opposite: MR JACK TROUNSON, 1924. Seen here in the garden of Laguna the Trounson family home, Jack is posing on his old James motorcycle. Over the years Jack had numerous motorcycles and invariably, fixed to the pillion seat, would be a wooden box in which would ride his pet dog.

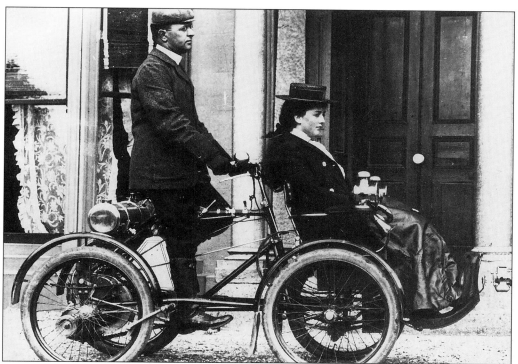

MR HARRY RICH, APRIL 1914. Although Harry Rich was known throughout the town for his association with the Wesleyan Chapel, he was also connected with the mining industry and was a great innovator. He very much enjoyed photography as well as driving all types of motorised vehicles. Here we see him with a very attractive lady riding an old Progress quadricycle number AF 77. It had a 2 Er HP De Dion engine and was completely open to the elements.

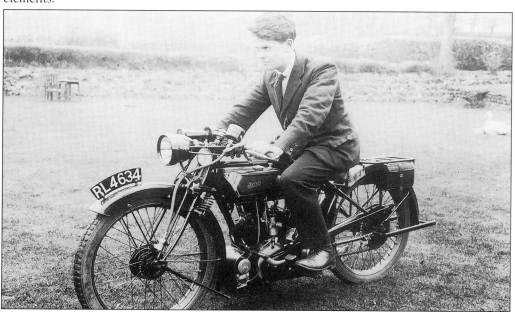

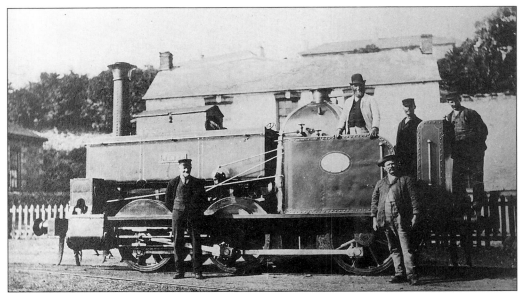

REDRUTH-CHACEWATER RAILWAY, 1880. Although this picture was taken at the terminus and engine sheds at Devoran, it shows the type of engine used between the Redruth terminus at St Day Road and Devoran Quay. One of three, Spitfire, Smelter and this one, Miner, were used to carry tin from Pednandrea Mine along the route through Trefusis Road, Pennance, Carharrack down into the Bissoe Valley, ending at the quays at Devoran. There are some places remaining where evidence of the old rail bed can be seen.

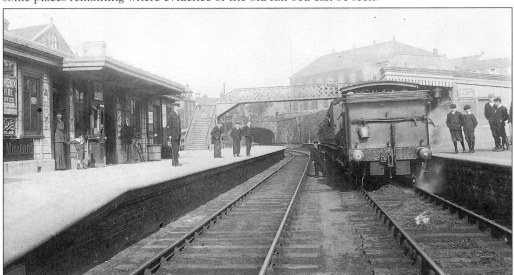

REDRUTH RAILWAY STATION, 1904. A view between the lines, with an old saddle tank engine on the "down" line ready to depart for Penzance. Note the "up" platform, which is relatively quiet at this time although, with the weekly exodus of miners emigrating to foreign parts, this was not always the scene. Over the years since it was first built (1843-44) the station has seen many changes including the installation of the iron bridge (1888), lengthening both platforms (1932), recovery of the sidings beside the down platform and shifting of the signal box from one end of the station to the other.

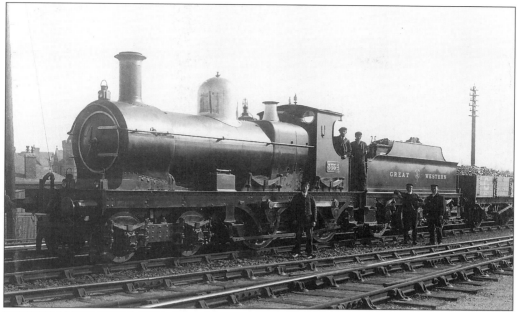

REDRUTH STATION, 1904. One of the engines that would have been seen operating at both Redruth and Drump Road stations during shunting work. This is No 3554 waiting at the "up" line for the signal to proceed.

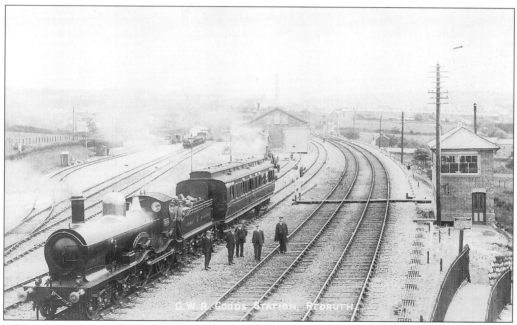

THE GOODS STATION, DRUMP ROAD, 1912. Because of increased trading in the area the G.W.R. decided to build a new Goods Station to replace the old buildings at Redruth Station. Just to the north of the existing station Drump Road goods depot was built. Here the old Bulldog class No. 3291 *Tregenna* waits opposite the new signal box with the engineers wagon, whilst testing operations are carried out.

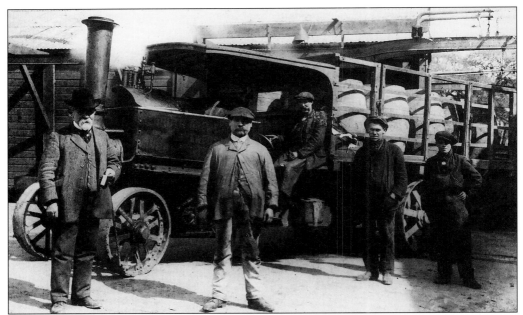

REDRUTH BREWERY STEAM WAGON, 1905. Having loaded up large barrels of beer at the brewery yard, this Foden Steam Wagon is ready to start on its delivery round.

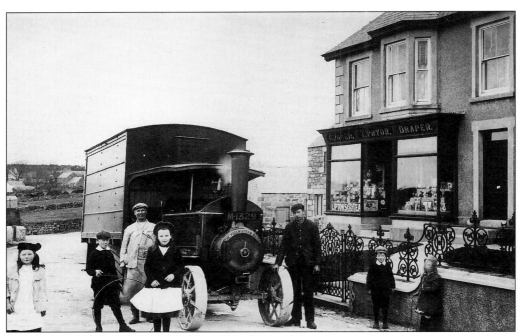

S, & T, TROUNSON STEAM WAGON, 1908. Although not taken in Redruth this shows S. & T. Trounson's Steam Foden No. M1329 *Pride of the West* delivering provisions to a shop at Carnkie, Wendron. The driver, Mr Ben Phillips, is on the left and a young 'Art' Pethick (about 18 yrs old) is on the right. Art was a legend where steam was concerned being involved with many local engines. His son, Donald, is carrying on his father's tradition.

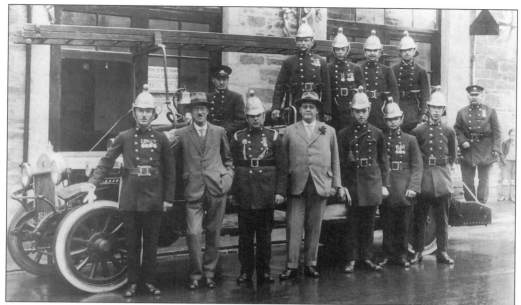

REDRUTH FIRE ENGINE, 1920. Redruth Fire Engine and crew stand outside the old Fire Station in Falmouth Road, having come into service around 1920. The vehicle, a Star 25 HP No. AF 1669 started life as a van for S. & T. Trounson but later was converted to the fire engine. The crew are, back row, left to right: 'Art' Pethick (Driver), Dick Troon, James Hailey, Percy Rogers, Tom Hill, Sam Trevena. Front row, left to right: Bill White, W. E. Shiers, Bert Dalymore (Captain), C. J. Cooke, Len Troon, R. Rogers, Tom Hart.

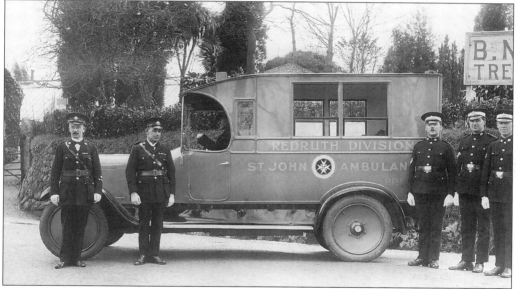

ST JOHNS AMBULANCE, 1930. Standing all resplendent at the top of Trewirgie Road outside Mr News Nurseries is the fairly new ambulance *Mercy*. This was only the second motorised ambulance Redruth Division had, replacing the old Hapmobile which had operated since 1919. Members of the brigade seen here are, left to right: Harry Pascoe, Supt. Lanyon, Joe Pengelly (Driver), Clifton Pellow, Stanley Seymour, Leslie Rowe.

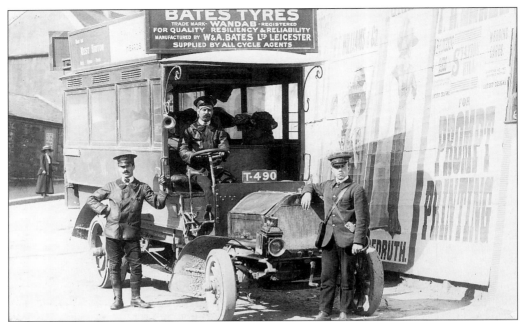

G.W.R. BUS, 1907. One of the very early G.W.R. buses, this one taken at Station Approach in July 1907 is waiting to leave for Falmouth. Pity the poor driver who would have to sit out in the open in all types of weather with only his leather jacket to keep him dry. Travelling to Falmouth must have been exciting with the solid tyres and carbide lamps! This particular vehicle, T490, was a Milnes-Daimler 20 HP which first came into service in the Paignton-Totnes area before being transferred to Redruth.

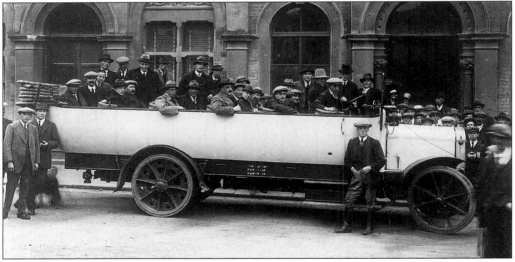

REDRUTH R.F.C., 1921. An away match in these days usually meant travelling by one of the local charabancs, this one, an old Thornycroft No. AF 2966, belonged to Williamsons of Camborne. This method of travel, what with solid tyres and indifferent road surfaces, did nothing to enhance the playing performance of the team, in this case an away match at Torquay. It was common for the body of such vehicles to be interchangeable and to have an open flat back for road haulage work.

Seven

Camborne-Redruth Tramway

It would be impossible during any discussion on transportation in the Camborne-Redruth area not to mention what was a unique method of travel. The system came into operation in November 1902 and worked until September 1927 with the mineral trams carrying on for a further six years. It was unique in two ways, firstly it was the only tramway in the County and secondly it was one of the few in the Country which allowed both passenger and mineral traffic over the same lines. What of the trams themselves? There were ten, eight passenger and two mineral and of the eight passengers, six were double deck type whilst the other two were single deck, similar to the American style. It is interesting to note that there are some thoughts of reopening the route with more modern type trams. The following photographs give some idea of the system, the route and the types of trams that worked over the lines from the terminus at Redruth through to Camborne.

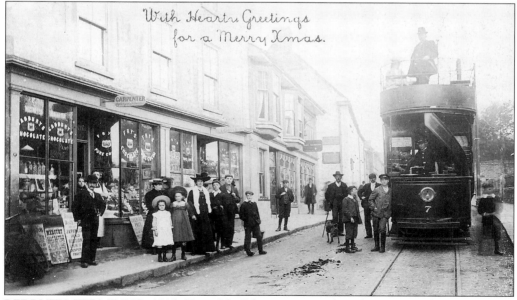

REDRUTH TERMINUS, 1905. Tram No 7 has just arrived at the West End terminus with driver E. Wallace at the controls. Carpenters Newsagents shop is on the left with advertisements showing the situation in the Russian-Japanese war. The next shop is the Tram terminus Tea and Coffee rooms.

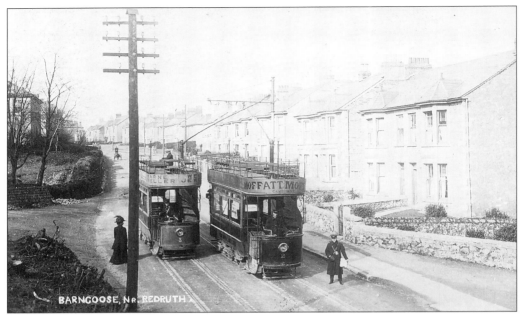

BARNCOOSE CROSSING LOOP, 1911. One of eight crossing loops, this one is outside Barncoose Hospital. Both trams show an absence of passengers. No 2 tram, heading towards Redruth, has a large parcel basket in the front. At this time trams were allowed to collect and carry post.

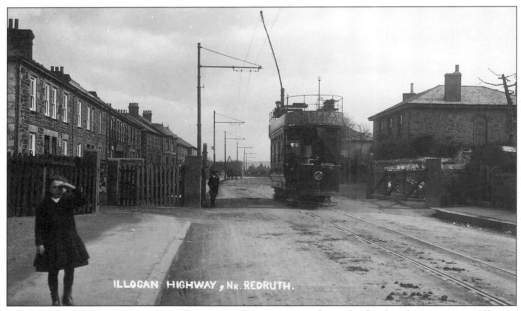

ILLOGAN HIGHWAY, 1912. Tram No 7 on its way through the level crossing at Illogan Highway. This railway line was the route from Carn Brea Station to Portreath carrying tin from the local mines down to the docks for shipping to the smelting works in Wales. The large building on the right is the Railway Inn.

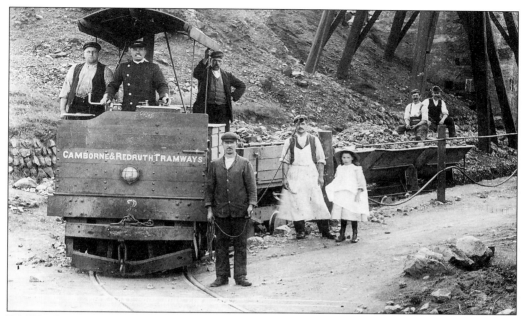

EAST POOL MINE, 1904. One of the two mineral trams, this is No 2, has just had its trucks loaded with tin ore and is about to leave Mitchells Shaft for the crushing plant at Tolvaddon. The driver is J. Williams and on his right is brakeman Bill Hampton.

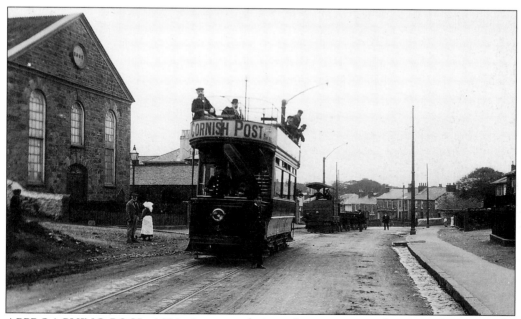

APPROACHING POOL, 1904. An unusual view of a passenger and a mineral tram on the same piece of track at the same time. Tram No 4 has just left Pool on its way to Redruth whilst the mineral tram is returning from the ore crushing plant at Tolvaddon. Note the Balmaiden on the left.

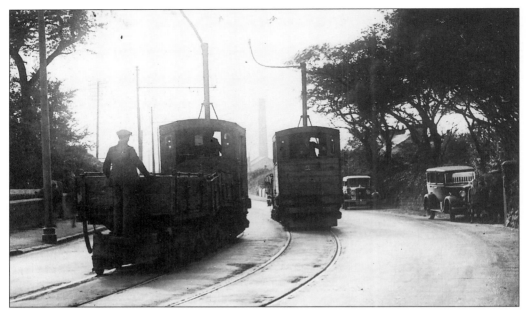

TREVENSON, 1920. The two mineral trams on the passing loop outside the entrance to what is now the Cornwall Technical College.

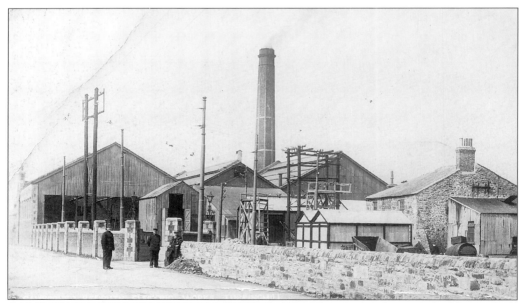

CAMBORNE-REDRUTH ELECTRIC WORKS, 1904. The source of power – buildings which housed the machinery to provide the electricity to operate the trams. Three generators were located in the centre of these buildings providing 480/530 volts DC. The building on the left is the tram shed and the one on the right is the boiler room.

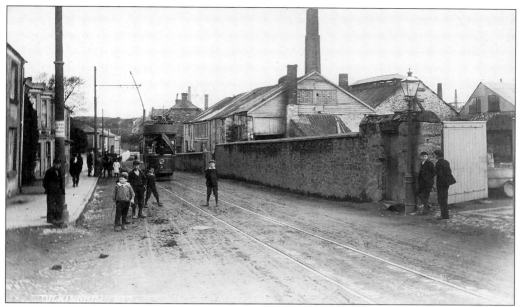

TUCKINGMILL, 1905. Outside the old Bickford Smith Dynamite and Fuse factory in Tuckingmill. Tram No 3 makes its way towards the steep climb up East Hill.

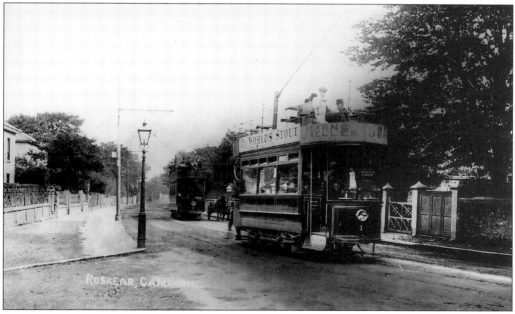

ROSKEAR LOOP, 1905. Trams No 1 and 2 on the passing loop at Roskear. It is interesting to see some of the advertisements that the trams displayed. Tram No 1 shows Wearnes the Jewellers and The Worlds Stout, Redruth Brewery Company.

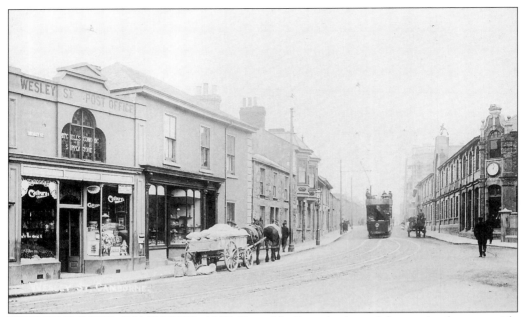

WESLEY STREET, CAMBORNE, 1907. Tram No 7 on the last of the passing loops outside what used to be the world famous Holmans Engineering Foundry. All the buildings on the right have now been demolished to make way for the new Tesco Store. The Post Office and the shops have long since closed.

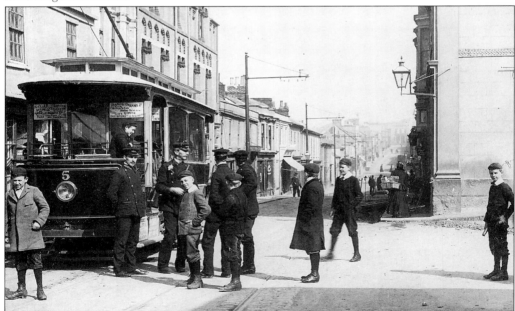

CAMBORNE TERMINUS, TRELOWARREN STREET, 1905. The end of the line – Trelowarren Street beside the old Commercial Hotel looking back down the long road towards Holmans Works. This picture shows one of the single deck trams. For some reason these vehicles were not very successful on this route, possibly it was something to do with the pick-up arm.

Eight

A Trip Around The District

Villages both large and small have grown out of all recognition since the early 1900s. Places which had a few cottages and a village store have seen the population increase through large residential developments. Their character has changed, more's the pity, although some have managed to retain their sense of community spirit.

With this last section of photographs I have tried to show what some of the villages around Redruth were like years ago. No doubt those people who lived and were brought up in these places will have their own special memories of days gone by.

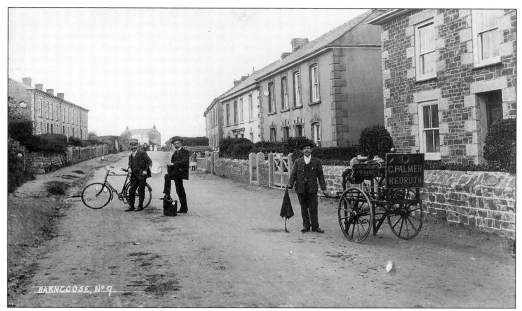

BARNCOOSE, 1904. Looking down Chariot Road from Rounding Walls, one of the roads which leads through Illogan to the beach at Portreath. No pavements in those days. Mr C. Palmer, a mobile umbrella repair man, is seen here with his handcart on his way around the area looking for trade.

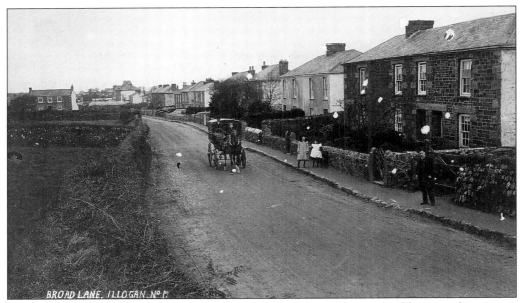

BROADLANE, 1905. Broadlane, an area which has changed considerably since this picture was taken. A new primary school and a large residential estate have been built alongside this road. The horse-drawn vehicle is that of Mr and Mrs Gilbert who ran the local bus service from Illogan to Redruth. The light fronted house to the right of the horse bus was where Thomas Merritt lived. Merritt was probably one of the best known people from this area, his musical prowess brought him universal success and his carols are still sung throughout the area at Christmas time.

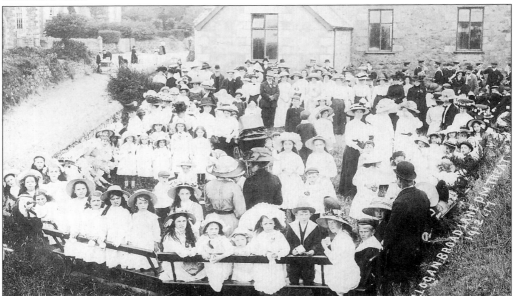

BROADLANE PRIMITIVE METHODIST CHAPEL, 1912. Members of the chapel gathered in the grounds of the Sunday School for the annual tea-treat. In the back left of the picture can be seen part of the main chapel. The photographer is standing on the old railway embankment of the Carn Brea to Portreath line.

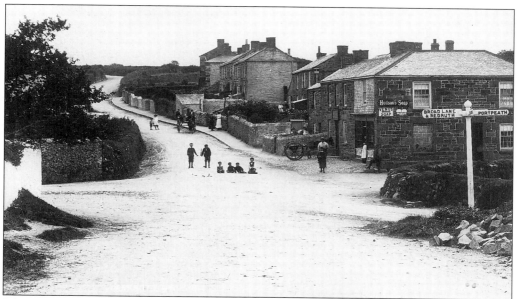

PARK BOTTOM, 1904. One of the smaller hamlets in the area which for some reason had no chapel or church although there were plenty in the surrounding district. Coming down the hill is the old road from Pool, now closed off for the new A30 dual carriageway. Park Bottom has not altered much over the years, there is still a shop on the corner and the New Inn is still open. Note the Donkey and Shay outside the entrance to the Inn waiting, no doubt, for its owner, Maggie Evans, to return.

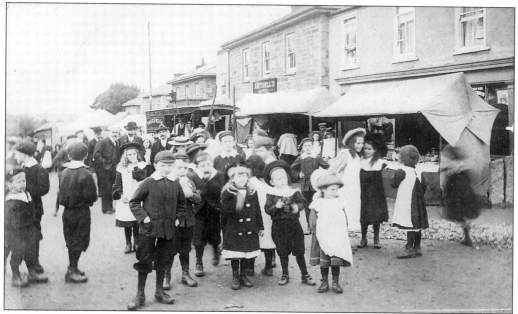

PAYNTERS LANE END, 1904. Over a mile from the turning at Rounding Walls is the area known as Paynters Lane End, about halfway to Portreath. Another village feast day is being celebrated with crowds turning out. Mr Tregenza with his Fish and Chip wagon is no doubt doing a roaring trade.

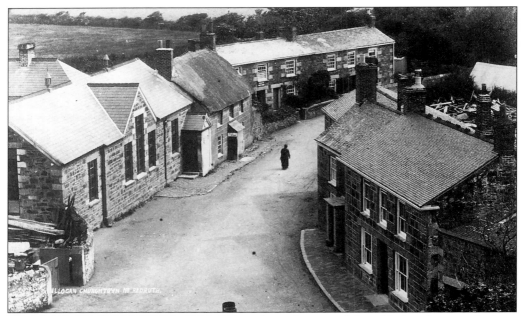

ILLOGAN CHURCHTOWN, 1904. Taken from the top of the old church tower looking down on a quiet rural scene. On the left is the Old Boys School followed by the thatched cottage of E. A. Bragg, a local photographer. It is through his photographs and postcards that so much of the social history of the area is known.

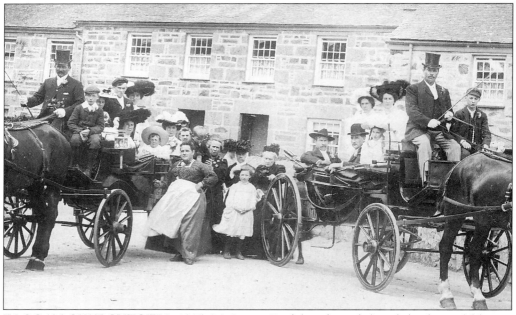

ILLOGAN CHURCHTOWN, 1905. Mr Jimmy Beal (on the right) with his beautiful horse-drawn landaus, perhaps just off to a wedding?

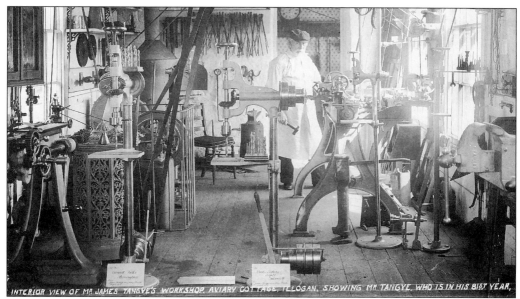

INTERIOR VIEW OF MR JAMES TANGYE'S WORKSHOP, AVIARY COTTAGE, ILLOGAN. SHOWING MR TANGYE, WHO IS IN HIS 81ST YEAR.

MR JAMES TANGYE'S WORKSHOP, 1906. One of the district's famous characters in his workshop at Aviary Cottage. James Tangye was an inventor and engineer of great renown. With his brother, Richard, and other members of the family he founded the great Cornwall Engineering Works in Birmingham. One of their inventions, an hydraulic jack, was helpful in launching one of the largest ships built in Britain, the *Great Eastern*. James Tangye is seen here in his workshop at the age of 81.

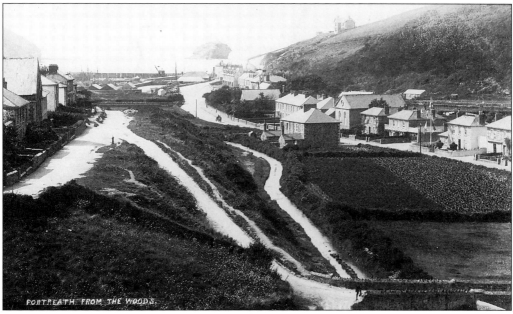

PORTREATH FROM THE WOODS.

PORTREATH, 1905. From Aviary Cottage down through Illogan Woods, the path leads out onto Primrose Terrace. From here can be seen the seaside village of Portreath with Gull rock in the distance.

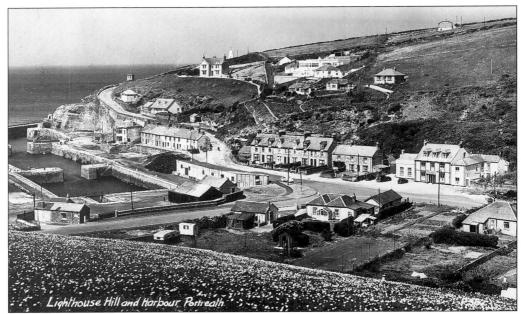

PORTREATH, 1950. A more modern view of part of the village with the harbour prominent on the left, a view we are unlikely to see again. Wherever you look changes have taken place – the harbour and old coal yard, the cottages in the foreground and the fields in the top right have all succumbed to modern developments.

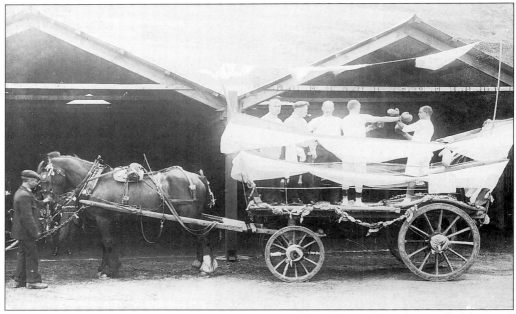

PORTREATH CARNIVAL, 1914. It was part of village life in these days to hold annual carnivals. Here we see one of the floats of the 1914 event and judging by the look of the boxers they are not budding Henry Coopers!

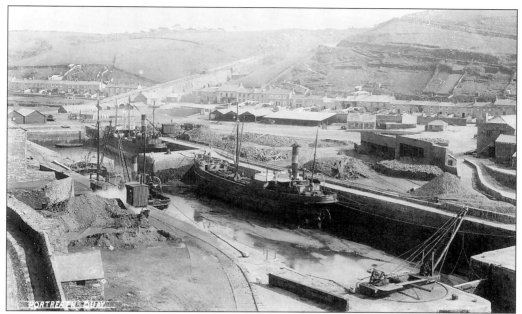

PORTREATH HARBOUR, 1905. A general view of the harbour with three small coastal steamers tied up after unloading their cargo of coal. The ships, *Olivia* on the left, *Treleigh* and *Guardian* on the right were part of the Bain Shipping Line that sailed between Portreath and Welsh ports taking minerals from the local mines for smelting and returning with coal. The harbour as seen here has been in existence since 1860 but there have been radical changes since the last steamer left here in 1960.

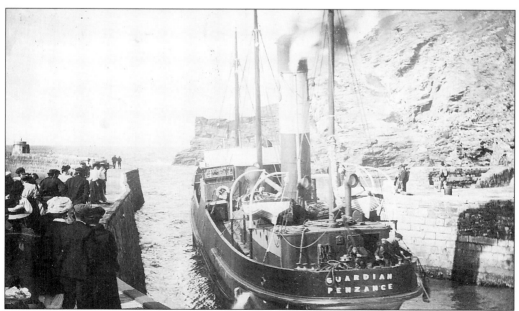

GUARDIAN LEAVING HARBOUR, 1908. A close-up view of the *Guardian* leaving the harbour. Conditions were fairly calm at the time but it was not always the case. When storms lash this part of the coast the exercise can be hazardous.

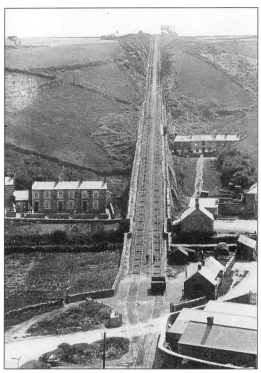

THE INCLINE, 1905. To enable coal and minerals to be carried to and from the mines it was decided to lay a branch line off the old Hayle railway between Carn Brea and Portreath. Almost the whole distance was over flat ground, however, to drop down into Portreath it was necessary to construct the incline seen here. With a gradient of 1 in 10, lowering and raising coal wagons was not easy, and so to assist in the operation a steam engine and winding gear were installed at the top of the incline using a steel hawser attached to the trucks.

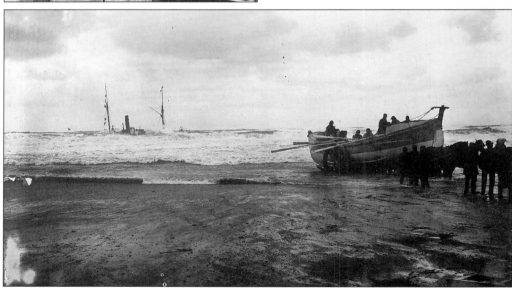

WRECK OF THE *ESCURIAL* 25 JANUARY, 1895. Over the years there have been many wrecks on this part of the North Cornwall coast but one that caught the public's imagination and sympathy was that of the S.S. *Escurial*. On her way from Cardiff to the continent, laden with coal, she developed engine problems causing her to be blown towards the shore and she eventually foundered. The local coastguards were unable to reach her, Hayle Lifeboat, which had been brought overland by a team of horses, could not be launched and by the time Newquay Lifeboat arrived it was too late. Of the nineteen crew only eight were saved.

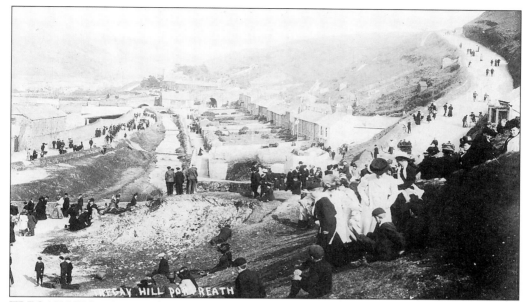

TREGAY HILL, 1910. Looking from the Battery Hill side of Portreath back to River Row and Tregay Hill. With so many people around it could be Easter weekend when one of the fairs would be set up on the Green (now the car park). The river running in front of the cottages was known as the Red River, due to the amount of tin flowing in the water from the mines of Redruth and Carnkie. The hill on the right leads to the coastal road to Hayle and St Ives and also the country mansion of the Bassett family at Tehidy.

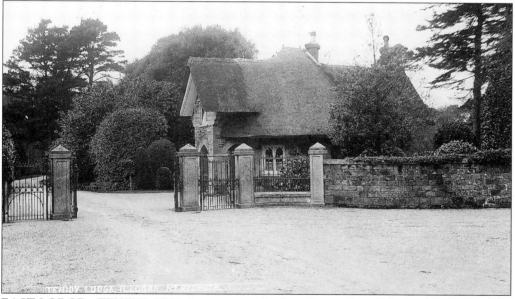

EAST LODGE - TEHIDY, 1904. Just over a mile from Portreath is Tehidy, the estate of the Bassett family. This lovely old lodge formed the eastern entrance and although the iron gates have gone, the lodge still stands, now in private ownership. The driveway took the visitor down through some woods and across the estate (now the Tehidy Park Golf Club) reaching the front courtyard of the house.

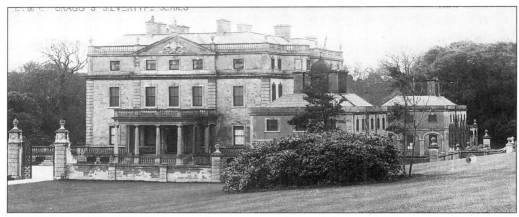

TEHIDY HOUSE, 1902. This magnificent country house, home to the Bassett family since the twelfth century, has seen many changes and alterations since its original construction. The building, as seen here, dates to around 1862. Since Arthur Bassett sold the bulk of the estate in 1919 the mansion was used mainly as a hospital but, unfortunately, even this has now closed and it has been put up for sale. What a beautiful monument to that particular period.

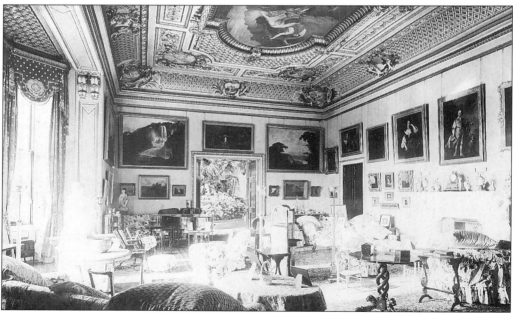

TEHIDY HOUSE - THE DRAWING ROOM. What a wonderful sight this must have been looking down through the drawing room towards the conservatory with the beautiful paintings and elegant furniture. Note the painting on the ceiling, seven Italian artists were commissioned to carry out the work.

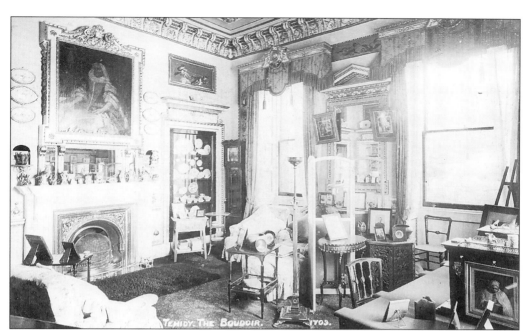

TEHIDY HOUSE - THE BOUDOIR. A peep inside one of the lady's bedrooms. After the conversion to a hospital this became a day room for nurses.

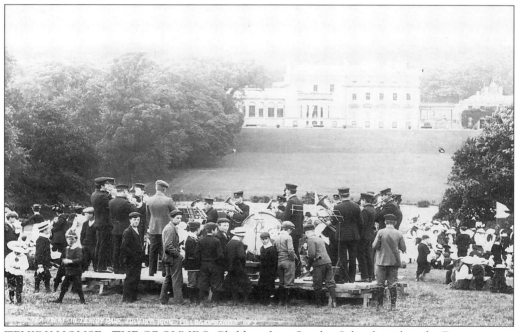

TEHIDY HOUSE - THE GROUNDS. Children from Sunday Schools within the Bassett estate area enjoyed their annual tea-treat in the field by the lake. The schools from the district paraded to the grounds by different routes, led by various bands. Once arrived games, races and rowing on the lake took place whilst music was provided by the Illogan Band conducted by the Revd Harry Oxland.

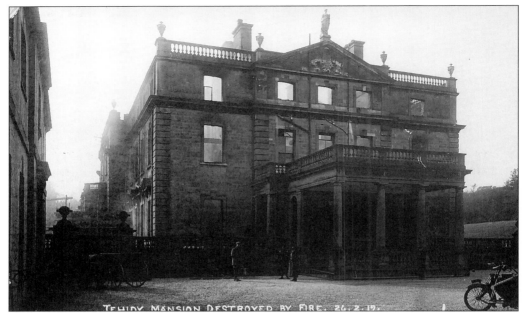

DESTROYED BY FIRE, 26 FEBRUARY 1919. During February 1918 Tehidy was handed over to Cornwall County Council for use as a sanatorium – by January 1919 work had been completed and the first patients were admitted. It was the end of the Bassett era, a tragedy, and as if in some form of protest a mysterious fire broke out and completely destroyed the inside of the building.

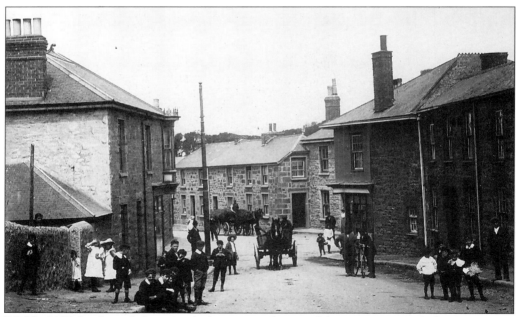

POOL, 1907. Looking down towards the crossroads at Pool from Station Road, the shop on the right corner was taken down many years ago for a road widening scheme. With the mines of East Pool and South Crofty close by, this was a very busy village.

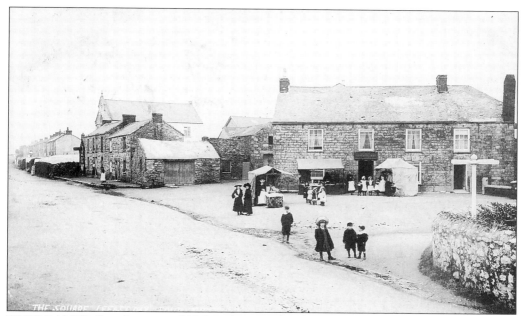

FOUR LANES. Standing some 700 feet above sea level this small village on the main Redruth to Helston road marks the southern boundary of the Bassett Estate. Here preparations are under way for the annual Feast Day. Some stalls have been erected including Granny Tresidders cockle stall, ready for the day's events to begin. The large building is the Victoria Inn, to the left is "Etchy" Williams' fish and chip shop and the bandroom.

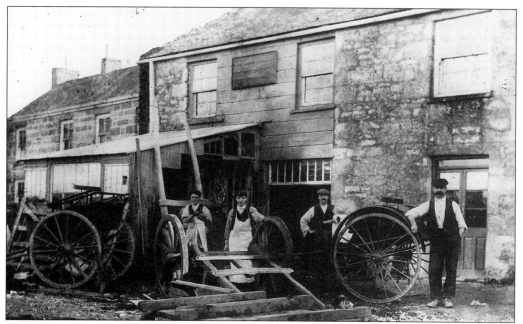

FOUR LANES - CARPENTERS SHOP, 1906. Near the crossroads was this old carpenter's shop owned by the Floyd family, left to right: Aubrey, Jack, Jim and Bill Floyd.

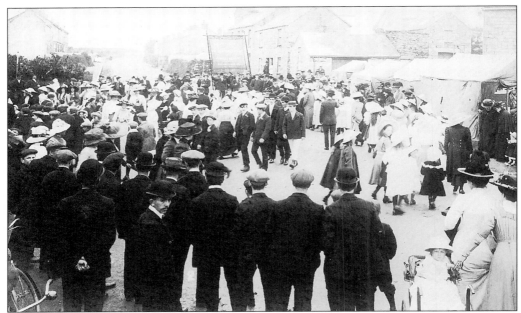

FOUR LANES SERPENTINE DANCE, 1910. One of the main attractions of the United Methodists Sunday School tea-treat was the Serpentine Dance. Members of the chapel would parade up and down the four roads of the village then, following the band, would form a column twisting and turning all around the square.

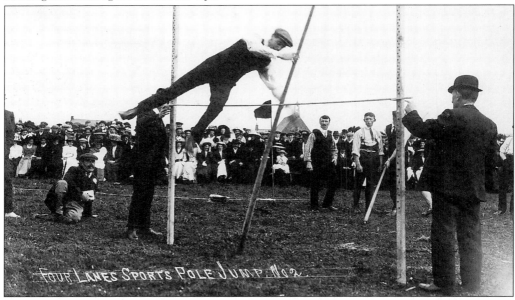

FOUR LANES ANNUAL SPORTS, 1910. Although not quite the Olympics, Four Lanes held one of the most popular athletics meetings when competitors would come from all over the County to take part. The events were held in fields opposite Pencoys Church – short sprints, five mile runs, walking events and as we see here, pole vaulting. Perhaps not the heights reached by today's athletes but, nevertheless, very exciting especially considering the dress of the competitors.

ROUGH STREET, LANNER. Rough Street was part of an early Roman road between Gwennap and St Michael's Mount used quite often by pilgrims. The bridge carried the track of the old railway to Tresavean Mine, part of the Hayle-Redruth line, branching off near Trevingey.

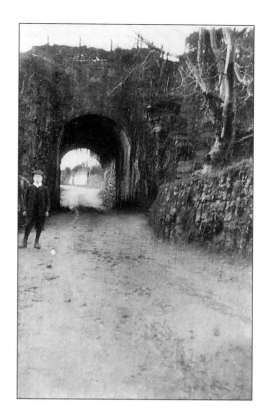

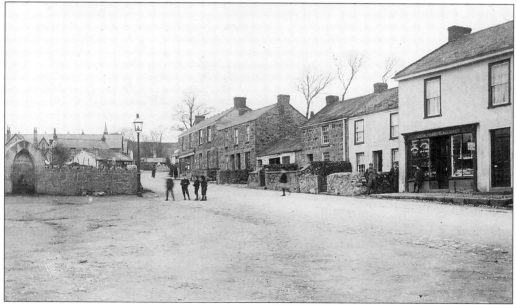

LANNER SQUARE, 1905. Looking from the Square towards what is now the very busy Redruth to Falmouth road. Mr Harry Veall's bakers shop is on the right, the small low building in the centre of the terrace was the old Blacksmith's Forge.

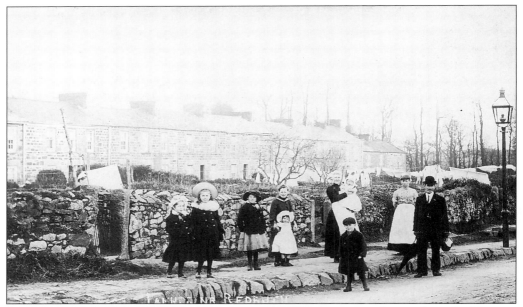

BEARS TERRACE, LANNER, 1908. A typical village scene, at the south end of Lanner village showing what would have been old miners cottages. Tresavean Mine was close by. Here some of the local population pose for the photographer.

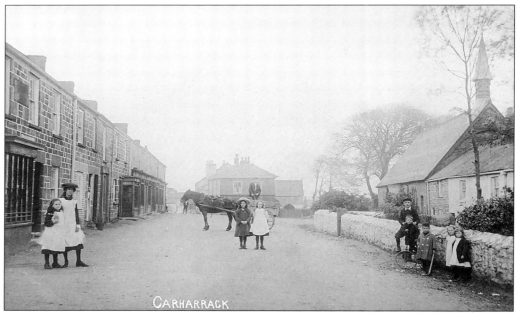

CARHARRACK, 1908. At one time Carharrack consisted of only twelve cottages but as more and more mines came into operation, so the village grew. Today it is an active and thriving community. On the right is the small church of St Piran, erected in 1884, and further down the road is the Bible Christian Chapel, built in memory of Billy Bray, the well known evangelist. At the rear of the houses on the left was the track of the Redruth and Chacewater railway.

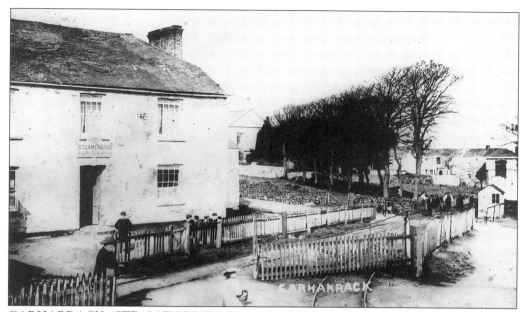

CARHARRACK - STEAM ENGINE INN, 1909. The Steam Engine Inn with part of the track of the Redruth to Chacewater railway. The line which ran from Trefusis Square in Redruth to Devoran was used purely for mineral traffic. The short branch line with the crossing gate was used to take coal into a small coalyard.

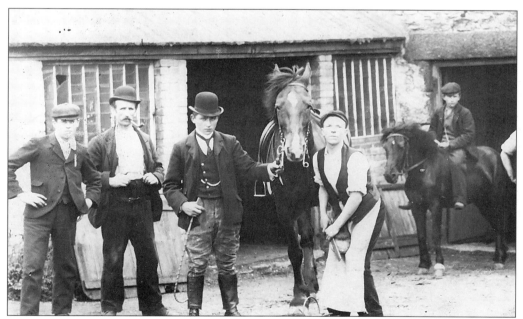

CARHARRACK - BLACKSMITH FORGE. One of the local farmers having his horse shod at Walter Lock's Forge. These premises were situated opposite the old Mills Hall.

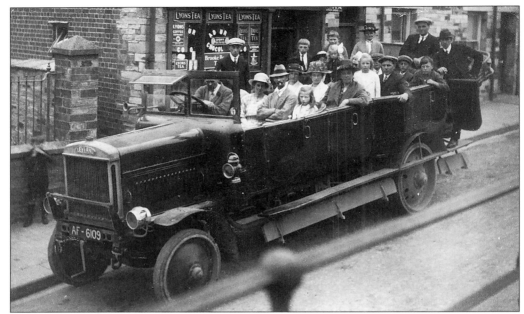

CARHARRACK WESLEYAN CHAPEL CHOIR, 1923. One of the highlights on the chapel's calendar was the annual outing of the choir. Here the Wesleyan chapel people are enjoying a trip to the Bodmin area. No doubt the experience of riding on this solid tyred Leyland charabanc was quite a novelty for the younger members. Some of the people seen here are: Harold Knuckey (driver), Albert Roberts (chapel organist), Pearl Lewis, Mr and Mrs Allen, Mr and Mrs Reg Burrows and the Gumma family.

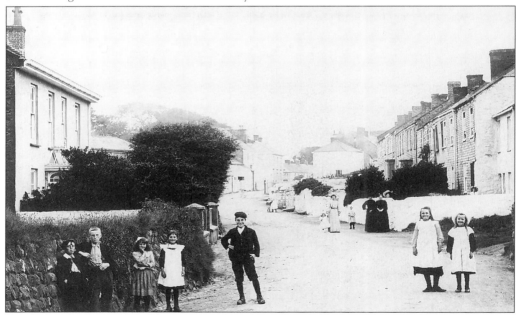

CARHARRACK - RAILWAY TERRACE, 1908. Local children posing for the photographer add charm to this idyllic village scene. This road leaving the village was so named because of the closeness of the Redruth and Chacewater line.

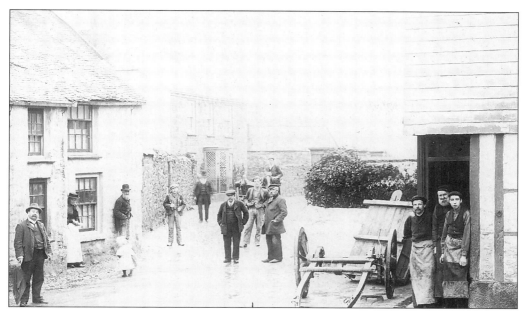

ST DAY WELL LANE, 1908. Entering St Day from Redruth at the west end of the village, this small side road was known as Well Lane, now Forth-an-Eglos. The house on the left is now used as the Community Centre. In the background is the old Wesleyan Manse and in the front Mr Eustice and his staff stand in the doorway of the carpenter's shop.

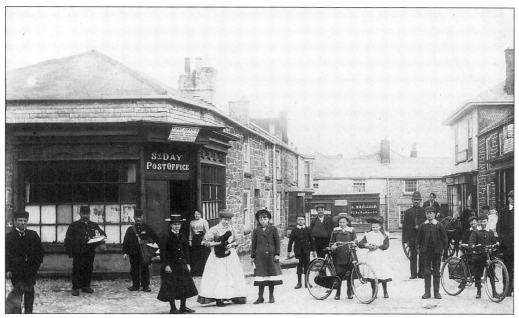

ST DAY, 1908. A lovely picture showing the centre of St Day and the old Post Office. The two postmen look ready to start on their daily deliveries whilst others are fascinated by the photographer. The local constable is P. C. Ough. St Day was known at one time as the "richest square mile in the county" because of the vast wealth produced from the local mines.

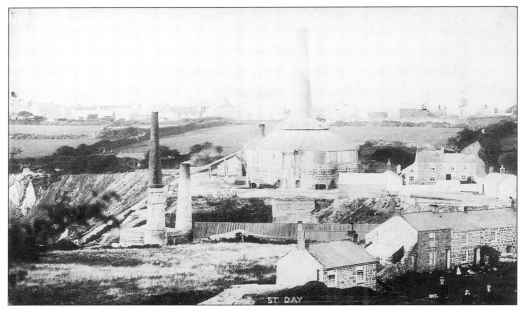

ST DAY BRICKWORKS, 1908. A general view of the St Day Brickworks with the large Hoffman kiln dominating the scene. On the left is the pit which provided the clay to make around 20,000 bricks per day, some of which can still be seen today, even though the works closed down in 1913.

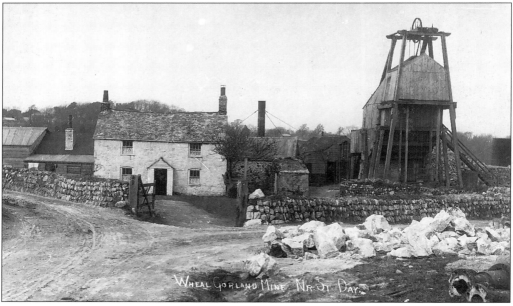

WHEAL GORLAND MINE, 1906. The headgear of Daveys Shaft and some of the mine buildings. An interesting feature of this particular mine was the great variety of minerals that were produced. Wheal Gorland started operating in the early 1800s, it closed in 1884 but reopened for a short period between 1905 and 1909, producing wolfram and black tin.

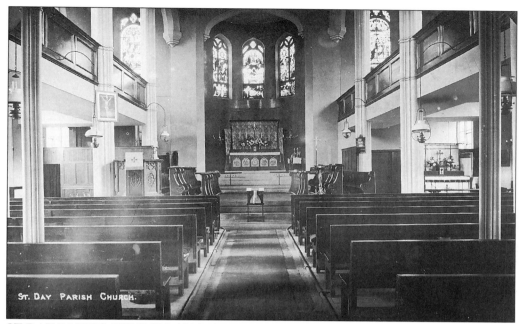

ST DAY PARISH CHURCH, 1904. A view not seen these days as it shows the interior of the old Parish Church which closed in 1956. Parts of pews and the old communion table were taken to the new church but there are many who mourn the loss of the old building.

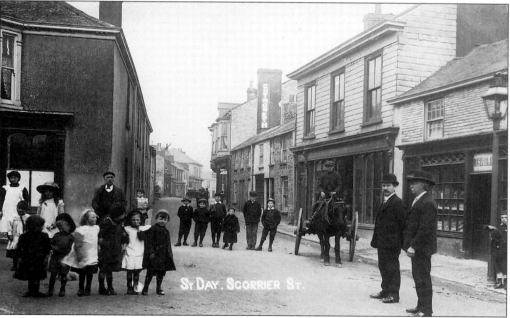

ST DAY - SCORRIER STREET, 1910. Looking along Scorrier Street today it appears to have altered very little from when this photograph was taken. The old paraffin street lamp and the horse-drawn water wagon have long gone, as have some of the shops. The larger shop on the right was that of T. R. Mills who acted as shipping agent for many of the miners who emigrated when the mines closed.

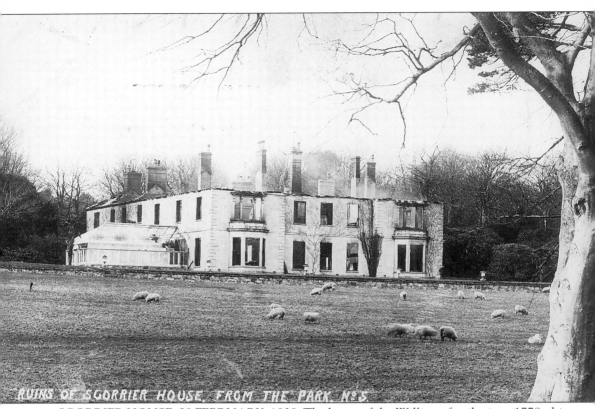

RUINS OF SCORRIER HOUSE. FROM THE PARK. N° 5.

SCORRIER HOUSE, 29 FEBRUARY, 1908. The home of the Williams family since 1778, this lovely country house was another that suffered badly from fire.

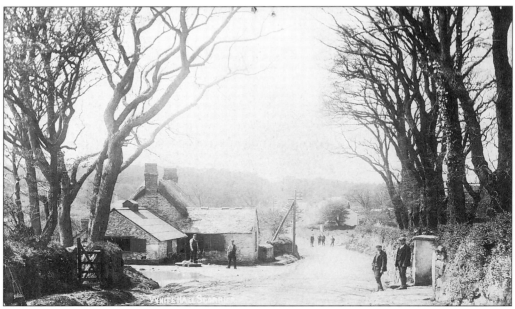

THE OLD BLACKSMITHS FORGE at Whitehall near Scorrier on the Redruth – Truro road.

Stock List

(Titles are listed according to the pre-1974 county boundaries)

BERKSHIRE

Wantage
Irene Hancock
ISBN 0-7524-0146 7

CARDIGANSHIRE

Aberaeron and Mid Ceredigion
William Howells
ISBN 0-7524-0106-8

CHESHIRE

Ashton-under-Lyne and Mossley
Alice Lock
ISBN 0-7524-0164-5

Around Bebington
Pat O'Brien
ISBN 0-7524-0121-1

Crewe
Brian Edge
ISBN 0-7524-0052-5

Frodsham and Helsby
Frodsham and District Local History Group
ISBN 0-7524-0161-0

Macclesfield Silk
Moira Stevenson and Louanne Collins
ISBN 0-7524-0315 X

Marple
Steve Cliffe
ISBN 0-7524-0316-8

Runcorn
Bert Starkey
ISBN 0-7524-0025-8

Warrington
Janice Hayes
ISBN 0-7524-0040-1

West Kirby to Hoylake
Jim O'Neil
ISBN 0-7524-0024-X

Widnes
Anne Hall and the Widnes Historical Society
ISBN 0-7524-0117-3

CORNWALL

Padstow
Malcolm McCarthy
ISBN 0-7524-0033-9

St Ives Bay
Jonathan Holmes
ISBN 0-7524-0186-6

COUNTY DURHAM

Bishop Auckland
John Land
ISBN 0-7524-0312-5

Around Shildon
Vera Chapman
ISBN 0-7524-0115-7

CUMBERLAND

Carlisle
Dennis Perriam
ISBN 0-7524-0166-1

DERBYSHIRE

Around Alfreton
Alfreton and District Heritage Trust
ISBN 0-7524-0041-X

Barlborough, Clowne, Creswell and Whitwell
Les Yaw
ISBN 0-7524-0031-2

Around Bolsover
Bernard Haigh
ISBN 0-7524-0021-5

Around Derby
Alan Champion and Mark Edworthy
ISBN 0-7524-0020-7

Long Eaton
John Barker
ISBN 0-7524-0110-6

Ripley and Codnor
David Buxton
ISBN 0-7524-0042-8

Shirebrook
Geoff Sadler
ISBN 0-7524-0028-2

Shirebrook: A Second Selection
Geoff Sadler
ISBN 0-7524-0317-6

DEVON

Brixham
Ted Gosling and Lyn Marshall
ISBN 0-7524-0037-1

Around Honiton
Les Berry and Gerald Gosling
ISBN 0-7524-0175-0

Around Newton Abbot
Les Berry and Gerald Gosling
ISBN 0-7524-0027-4

Around Ottery St Mary
Gerald Gosling and Peter Harris
ISBN 0-7524-0030-4

Around Sidmouth
Les Berry and Gerald Gosling
ISBN 0-7524-0137-8

DORSET

Around Uplyme and Lyme Regis
Les Berry and Gerald Gosling
ISBN 0-7524-0044-4

ESSEX

Braintree and Bocking
John and Sandra Adlam and Mark Charlton
ISBN 0-7524-0129-7

Ilford
Ian Dowling and Nick Harris
ISBN 0-7524-0050-9

Ilford: A Second Selection
Ian Dowling and Nick Harris
ISBN 0-7524-0320-6

Saffron Walden
Jean Gumbrell
ISBN 0-7524-0176-9

GLAMORGAN

Around Bridgend
Simon Eckley
ISBN 0-7524-0189-0

Caerphilly
Simon Eckley
ISBN 0-7524-0194-7

Around Kenfig Hill and Pyle
Keith Morgan
ISBN 0-7524-0314-1

The County Borough of Merthyr Tydfil
Carolyn Jacob, Stephen Done and Simon Eckley
ISBN 0-7524-0012-6

Mountain Ash, Penrhiwceiber and Abercynon
Bernard Baldwin and Harry Rogers
ISBN 0-7524-0114-9

Pontypridd
Simon Eckley
ISBN 0-7524-0017-7

Rhondda
Simon Eckley and Emrys Jenkins
ISBN 0-7524-0028-2

Rhondda: A Second Selection
Simon Eckley and Emrys Jenkins
ISBN 0-7524-0308-7

Roath, Splott, and Adamsdown
Roath Local History Society
ISBN 0-7524-0199-8

GLOUCESTERSHIRE

Barnwood, Hucclecote and Brockworth
Alan Sutton
ISBN 0-7524-0000-2

Forest to Severn
Humphrey Phelps
ISBN 0-7524-0008-8

Filton and the Flying Machine
Malcolm Hall
ISBN 0-7524-0171-8

Gloster Aircraft Company
Derek James
ISBN 0-7524-0038-X

The City of Gloucester
Jill Voyce
ISBN 0-7524-0306-0

Around Nailsworth and Minchinhampton from the Conway Collection
Howard Beard
ISBN 0-7524-0048-7

Around Newent
Tim Ward
ISBN 0-7524-0003-7

Stroud: Five Stroud Photographers
Howard Beard, Peter Harris and Wilf Merrett
ISBN 0-7524-0305-2

HAMPSHIRE

Gosport
Ian Edelman
ISBN 0-7524-0300-1

Winchester from the Sollars Collection
John Brimfield
ISBN 0-7524-0173-4

HEREFORDSHIRE

Ross-on-Wye
Tom Rigby and Alan Sutton
ISBN 0-7524-0002-9

HERTFORDSHIRE

Buntingford
Philip Plumb
ISBN 0-7524-0170-X

Hampstead Garden Suburb
Mervyn Miller
ISBN 0-7524-0319-2

Hemel Hempstead
Eve Davis
ISBN 0-7524-0167-X

Letchworth
Mervyn Miller
ISBN 0-7524-0318-4

Welwyn Garden City
Angela Eserin
ISBN 0-7524-0133-5

KENT

Hythe
Joy Melville and Angela Lewis-Johnson
ISBN 0-7524-0169-6

North Thanet Coast
Alan Kay
ISBN 0-7524-0112-2

Shorts Aircraft
Mike Hooks
ISBN 0-7524-0193-9

LANCASHIRE

Lancaster and the Lune Valley
Robert Alston
ISBN 0-7524-0015-0

Morecambe Bay
Robert Alston
ISBN 0-7524-0163-7

Manchester
Peter Stewart
ISBN 0-7524-0103-3

LINCOLNSHIRE

Louth
David Cuppleditch
ISBN 0-7524-0172-6

Stamford
David Gerard
ISBN 0-7524-0309-5

LONDON
(Greater London and Middlesex)

Battersea and Clapham
Patrick Loobey
ISBN 0-7524-0010-X

Canning Town
Howard Bloch and Nick Harris
ISBN 0-7524-0057-6

Chiswick
Carolyn and Peter Hammond
ISBN 0-7524-0001-0

Forest Gate
Nick Harris and Dorcas Sanders
ISBN 0-7524-0049-5

Greenwich
Barbara Ludlow
ISBN 0-7524-0045-2

Highgate and Muswell Hill
Joan Schwitzer and Ken Gay
ISBN 0-7524-0119-X

Islington
Gavin Smith
ISBN 0-7524-0140-8

Lewisham
John Coulter and Barry Olley
ISBN 0-7524-0059-2

Leyton and Leytonstone
Keith Romig and Peter Lawrence
ISBN 0-7524-0158-0

Newham Dockland
Howard Bloch
ISBN 0-7524-0107-6

Norwood
Nicholas Reed
ISBN 0-7524-0147-5

Peckham and Nunhead
John D. Beasley
ISBN 0-7524-0122-X

Piccadilly Circus
David Oxford
ISBN 0-7524-0196-3

Stoke Newington
Gavin Smith
ISBN 0-7524-0159-9

Sydenham and Forest Hill
John Coulter and John Seaman
ISBN 0-7524-0036-3

Wandsworth
Patrick Loobey
ISBN 0-7524-0026-6

Wanstead and Woodford
Ian Dowling and Nick Harris
ISBN 0-7524-0113-0

MONMOUTHSHIRE

Vanished Abergavenny
Frank Olding
ISBN 0-7524-0034-7

Abertillery, Aberbeeg and Llanhilleth
Abertillery and District Museum Society and Simon Eckley
ISBN 0-7524-0134-3

Blaina, Nantyglo and Brynmawr
Trevor Rowson
ISBN 0-7524-0136-X

NORFOLK

North Norfolk
Cliff Richard Temple
ISBN 0-7524-0149-1

NOTTINGHAMSHIRE

Nottingham 1897–1947
Douglas Whitworth
ISBN 0-7524-0157-2

OXFORDSHIRE

Banbury
Tom Rigby
ISBN 0-7524-0013-4

PEMBROKESHIRE

Saundersfoot and Tenby
Ken Daniels
ISBN 0-7524-0192-0

RADNORSHIRE

Llandrindod Wells
Chris Wilson
ISBN 0-7524-0191-2

SHROPSHIRE

Leominster
Eric Turton
ISBN 0-7524-0307-9

Ludlow
David Lloyd
ISBN 0-7524-0155-6

Oswestry
Bernard Mitchell
ISBN 0-7524-0032-0

North Telford: Wellington, Oakengates, and Surrounding Areas
John Powell and Michael A. Vanns
ISBN 0-7524-0124-6

South Telford: Ironbridge Gorge, Madeley, and Dawley
John Powell and Michael A. Vanns
ISBN 0-7524-0125-4

SOMERSET

Bath
Paul De'Ath
ISBN 0-7524-0127-0

Around Yeovil
Robin Ansell and Marion Barnes
ISBN 0-7524-0178-5

STAFFORDSHIRE

Cannock Chase
Sherry Belcher and Mary Mills
ISBN 0-7524-0051-7

Around Cheadle
George Short
ISBN 0-7524-0022-3

The Potteries
Ian Lawley
ISBN 0-7524-0046-0

East Staffordshire
Geoffrey Sowerby and Richard Farman
ISBN 0-7524-0197-1

SUFFOLK

Lowestoft to Southwold
Humphrey Phelps
ISBN 0-7524-0108-4

Walberswick to Felixstowe
Humphrey Phelps
ISBN 0-7524-0109-2

SURREY

Around Camberley
Ken Clarke
ISBN 0-7524-0148-3

Around Cranleigh
Michael Miller
ISBN 0-7524-0143-2

Epsom and Ewell
Richard Essen
ISBN 0-7524-0111-4

Farnham by the Wey
Jean Parratt
ISBN 0-7524-0185-8

Industrious Surrey: Historic Images of the County at Work
Chris Shepheard
ISBN 0-7524-0009-6

Reigate and Redhill
Mary G. Goss
ISBN 0-7524-0179-3

Richmond and Kew
Richard Essen
ISBN 0-7524-0145-9

SUSSEX

Billingshurst
Wendy Lines
ISBN 0-7524-0301-X

WARWICKSHIRE

Central Birmingham 1870–1920
Keith Turner
ISBN 0-7524-0053-3

Old Harborne
Roy Clarke
ISBN 0-7524-0054-1

WILTSHIRE

Malmesbury
Dorothy Barnes
ISBN 0-7524-0177-7

Great Western Swindon
Tim Bryan
ISBN 0-7524-0153-X

Midland and South Western Junction Railway
Mike Barnsley and Brian Bridgeman
ISBN 0-7524-0016-9

WORCESTERSHIRE

Around Malvern
Keith Smith
ISBN 0-7524-0029-0

YORKSHIRE
(EAST RIDING)

Hornsea
G.L. Southwell
ISBN 0-7524-0120-3

YORKSHIRE
(NORTH RIDING)

Northallerton
Vera Chapman
ISBN 0-7524-055-X

Scarborough in the 1970s and 1980s
Richard Percy
ISBN 0-7524-0325-7

YORKSHIRE
(WEST RIDING)

Barnsley
Barnsley Archive Service
ISBN 0-7524-0188-2

Bingley
Bingley and District Local History Society
ISBN 0-7524-0311-7

Bradford
Gary Firth
ISBN 0-7524-0313-3

Castleford
Wakefield Metropolitan District Council
ISBN 0-7524-0047-9

Doncaster
Peter Tuffrey
ISBN 0-7524-0162-9

Harrogate
Malcolm Neesam
ISBN 0-7524-0154-8

Holme Valley
Peter and Iris Bullock
ISBN 0-7524-0139-4

Horsforth
Alan Cockroft and Matthew Young
ISBN 0-7524-0130-0

Knaresborough
Arnold Kellett
ISBN 0-7524-0131-9

Around Leeds
Matthew Young and Dorothy Payne
ISBN 0-7524-0168-8

Penistone
Matthew Young and David Hambleton
ISBN 0-7524-0138-6

Selby from the William Rawling Collection
Matthew Young
ISBN 0-7524-0198-X

Central Sheffield
Martin Olive
ISBN 0-7524-0011-8

Around Stocksbridge
Stocksbridge and District History Society
ISBN 0-7524-0165-3

TRANSPORT

Filton and the Flying Machine
Malcolm Hall
ISBN 0-7524-0171-8

Gloster Aircraft Company
Derek James
ISBN 0-7524-0038-X

Great Western Swindon
Tim Bryan
ISBN 0-7524-0153-X

Midland and South Western Junction Railway
Mike Barnsley and Brian Bridgeman
ISBN 0-7524-0016-9

Shorts Aircraft
Mike Hooks
ISBN 0-7524-0193-9

This stock list shows all titles available in the United Kingdom as at 30 September 1995.

ORDER FORM

The books in this stock list are available from your local bookshop. Alternatively they are available by mail order at a totally inclusive price of £10.00 per copy.

For overseas orders please add the following postage supplement for each copy ordered:

>   European Union £0.36 (this includes the Republic of Ireland)
>   Royal Mail Zone 1 (for example, U.S.A. and Canada) £1.96
>   Royal Mail Zone 2 (for example, Australia and New Zealand) £2.47

Please note that all of these supplements are actual Royal Mail charges with no profit element to the Chalford Publishing Company. Furthermore, as the Air Mail Printed Papers rate applies, we are restricted from enclosing any personal correspondence other than to indicate the senders name.

Payment can be made by cheque, Visa or Mastercard. Please indicate your method of payment on this order form.

If you are not entirely happy with your purchase you may return it within 30 days of receipt for a full refund.

Please send your order to:

>   The Chalford Publishing Company,
>   St Mary's Mill,
>   Chalford,
>   Stroud,
>   Gloucestershire
>   GL6 8NX

This order form should perforate away from the book. However, if you are reluctant to damage the book in any way we are quite happy to accept a photocopy order form or a letter containing the necessary information.

PLEASE WRITE CLEARLY USING BLOCK CAPITALS

Name and address of the person ordering the books listed below:

_____

_____   _____

_____   Post code _____

Please also supply your telephone number in case we have difficulty fully understanding your requirements.   Tel.: _____ - _____

Name and address of where the books are to be despatched to (if different from above):

_____

_____

_____   Post code _____

Please indicate here if you would like to receive future information on books published by the Chalford Publishing Company.

____ Yes, please put me on your mailing list   ____ No, please just send the books ordered below

Title	ISBN	Quantity
....	0-7524-_____-___	_____
....	0-7524-_____-___	_____
....	0-7524-_____-___	_____
....	0-7524-_____-___	_____
....	0-7524-_____-___	_____
	Total number of books	_____

Cost of books delivered in UK = Number of books ordered @ £10 each =£ _____

Overseas postage supplement (if relevant) · =£ _____

TOTAL PAYMENT =£ _____

Method of Payment   ❑ Cheque   ❑ Visa   ❑ Mastercard   **VISA**

Please make cheques payable to *The Chalford Publishing Company*   MasterCard

Name of Card Holder   _____

Card Number ❑❑❑❑❑❑❑❑❑❑❑❑❑❑❑❑❑❑❑

Expiry date ❑❑ / ❑❑

I authorise payment of £_____ from the above card

Signed _____